LIGUORI CHRISTIAN INITIATION PRO

Journey of Faith

FOR CHILDREN

CATECHUMENATE LEADER GUIDE

Liguori PUBLICATIONS
A Redemptorist Ministry

CATECHUMENATE

JOURNEY OF FAITH

Journey of Faith for Children, Catechumenate Leader Guide (827181)

Imprimi Potest: Stephen T. Rehrauer, CSsR, Provincial, Denver Province, the Redemptorists

Imprimatur: "In accordance with CIC 827, permission to publish has been granted on March 20, 2017, by Bishop-Elect Mark S. Rivituso, Vicar General, Archdiocese of St. Louis. Permission to publish is an indication that nothing contrary to Church teaching is contained in this work. It does not imply any endorsement of the opinions expressed in the publication, nor is any liability assumed by this permission."

Journey of Faith © 1993, 2005, 2017 Liguori Publications, Liguori, MO 63057.
To order, visit Liguori.org or call 800-325-9521.

Liguori Publications, a nonprofit corporation, is an apostolate of the Redemptorists. To learn more about the Redemptorists, visit Redemptorists.com. All rights reserved. No part of this publication may be reproduced, distributed, stored, transmitted, or posted in any form by any means without prior written permission.

Text: Adapted from *Journey of Faith for Adults* © 2000 Liguori Publications.

Editor of the 2017 *Journey of Faith for Children*: Theresa Nienaber-Panuski.
Design and production: Wendy Barnes, Lorena Mitre Jimenez, John Krus, and Bill Townsend.
Cover image: Soloviova Liudmyla/Shutterstock. Interior illustration: Jeff Albrecht.

Unless noted, Scripture texts in this work are taken from the *New American Bible*, revised edition © 2000, 1991, 1986, 1970 Confraternity of Christian Doctrine, Washington, D.C., and are used by permission of the copyright owner. All Rights Reserved. No part of the *New American Bible* may be reproduced in any form without permission in writing from the copyright owner.

Excerpts from the English translation of the *Catechism of the Catholic Church* for the United States of America © 1994 United States Catholic Conference, Inc.—*Libreria Editrice Vaticana*; English translation of the *Catechism of the Catholic Church: Modifications from the Editio Typica* © 1997 United States Catholic Conference, Inc.—*Libreria Editrice Vaticana*.

Excerpts from *The Rites of the Catholic Church, Volume One* (abbreviated *RCIA* herein) © 1990 Liturgical Press.

Compliant with *The Roman Missal, Third Edition*.

Printed in the United States of America
21 20 19 18   / 5 4 3 2
Third Edition

Contents

**The Catechumenate:
A Period and Process** 4

Rites Belonging to the Catechumenate 5

Sponsors and Godparents:
Knowing and Making the Difference 7

Effective Catechesis During the Catechumenate 7

Practical Suggestions 8

Integrating the Parish Community 9

Catechumenate Lesson Plans 10

C1. The RCIA Process and Rites

C2. The Sacraments: An Introduction

C3. The Sacrament of Baptism

C4. The Sacrament of Confirmation

C5. The Sacrament of the Eucharist

C6. The Sacrament of Penance and Reconciliation

C7. The Sacrament of Anointing of the Sick

C8. The Sacrament of Matrimony

C9. The Sacrament of Holy Orders

C10. The People of God

C11. The Early Church

C12. Church History

C13. Living Like Jesus Today

C14. Caring for All God's Creatures

C15. Choose Life Always

C16. Caring for God's Community

Catechumenate Glossary 106

The Catechumenate: A Period and a Process

Since the time of the early Church, generally "the catechumenate" referred to the entire process of Christian conversion and initiation. It spanned multiple years and involved formal instruction, acts of penitence, and public rites that confirmed the community's approval as well as the catechumen's changed status.

Today, *catechumenate*, and *catechumen* in some respects, refers to a specific stage within the typical RCIA process. The rite of acceptance has been called a "first step," even though most participants take part in a period of inquiry as well as unknown years of personal discernment before contacting a Catholic parish (*RCIA* 42). While the rite of election technically "closes the period of the catechumenate proper," catechumens (then the *elect*) and candidates continue to meet for months and have not yet been fully initiated (*RCIA* 118; see also *National Statutes for the Catechumenate*, 6).

The period of the catechumenate remains at the heart of the RCIA process. Team members, catechists, and participants should take advantage of all its benefits and allow it to progress naturally. Especially when an inquirer enters the process later than others, Lent arrives early, or there are exceptional circumstances, it may be best to extend the length of this period rather than rushing through or shortchanging the participant's needs and experiences.

While the catechumenate is distinctly reserved for more formal instruction and presentation of essential doctrine, it is also a time for participants to practice and apply their faith. The Church identifies four goals for the catechumenate (*RCIA* 75). During this period, participants will:

1. receive a "suitable catechesis…planned to be gradual and complete in its coverage….This catechesis leads the catechumens not only to an appropriate acquaintance with dogmas and precepts but also to a profound sense of the mystery of salvation…" (see also the Decree on the Church's Missionary Activity [*Ad Gentes*], 14, from the Second Vatican Council documents).

2. "become familiar with the Christian way of life…, learn to turn more readily to God in prayer, …and to practice love of neighbor, even at the cost of self-renunciation."

3. participate in "suitable liturgical rites, which purify the catechumens little by little and strengthen them with God's blessing…. At Mass they may also take part with the faithful in the Liturgy of the Word, thus better preparing themselves for their eventual participation in the liturgy of the Eucharist."

4. "learn how to work actively with others to spread the Gospel and build up the Church.…"

Throughout the catechumenate, catechumens and candidates will undergo "a progressive change of outlook and morals" (*AG* 13). RCIA leaders and sponsors can be catalysts for this spiritual transformation by providing opportunities for reflection, interaction with the community, and by supporting their study with clear and accurate information. Many features of the *Journey of Faith* program and materials assist you in achieving those goals.

Prior to the rite of election, leaders, sponsors, and participants themselves should observe an increase in the participant's understanding and ownership of his or her Catholic Christian faith. The signing of names into the *Book of the Elect* signifies the fuller "yes" to Christ and Church that began in his or her heart at the rite of acceptance.

Rites Belonging to the Catechumenate

Celebrations of the Word of God

The catechumenate, indeed the entire RCIA process, is connected intrinsically to the liturgical year. The Church recommends that it last at least one year to ensure that catechumens experience the fullness of the paschal mystery as reflected in the liturgy.

Many RCIA groups attend the Sunday Liturgy of the Word together. Others meet during the week to proclaim and reflect on the upcoming readings. You may combine these celebrations with the catechetical sessions or keep them separate. However you structure your RCIA process, maintaining a connection to the seasons of the Church year and regularly, prayerfully breaking open the Scriptures is vitally important.

Model for a Celebration of the Word of God

1. *Song.* The celebration opens with an appropriate hymn or chant.

2. *Readings and Responsorial Psalm.* A baptized member, ideally a trained lector, proclaims a reading or two from Scripture. As in Mass, the first or Old Testament readings are followed by a psalm, either sung or in a call-and-response format.

3. *Lesson.* The RCIA director, pastor, or another trained catechist briefly explains and applies the readings.

4. *Concluding Rites.* The celebration closes with a prayer or one or more of the optional rites below (*RCIA* 85–89).

Optional Rites

Catechumens and candidates can be nourished by other liturgical rites during this period. The Church offers texts and guidelines for minor exorcisms (petitions for strength in the challenges of faith and struggle against temptation), blessings, and anointings, which may occur on their own or conclude a celebration of the word (*RCIA* 90–103). Speak to your priest or deacon about when and how these might benefit your group.

Also, you will need to determine what rites are appropriate for the period of enlightenment and how they will fit into the weeks leading up to the Easter Vigil. The Presentations of the Creed and Lord's Prayer can be moved to late in the catechumenate if necessary, but the priest, deacon, or director of religious education (DRE) should ensure that the catechumens are ready beforehand.

If the rites of election and/or calling are celebrated by the bishop elsewhere in the diocese, both the parish and participants will benefit from the rite of sending. In this rite, the local pastor and community preliminarily approve and celebrate the participants' readiness (see *RCIA* 106–17, 434–45, 530–46). It demonstrates their present, though distant, love and support and strengthens the catechumens and candidates for their return and entrance into the Lenten season.

The Rite of Election

The rite of election is a major milestone in the catechumens' RCIA journey. Usually occurring on the first Sunday of Lent, they publicly pledge their fidelity to the Church and sign the *Book of the Elect*. Baptized candidates participate in the rite of calling the candidates to continuing conversion or in a combined rite. These rites are very similar but do not include any signing.

The *Journey of Faith* program provides a basic outline to the rite of election in lesson *C1: The RCIA Process and Rites* and spiritual preparation through Scripture and reflection in lesson *E1: Saying Yes to Jesus.*

"Before the rite of election the bishop, priests, deacons, catechists, godparents, and the entire community [should] arrive at a judgment about the catechumens' state of formation and progress" (*RCIA* 121). This doesn't mean an interview or exam is needed. However, pastors who have not attended the RCIA sessions may want to speak briefly to you about the group.

This is a good time to gather the team members' and sponsors' feedback and experiences with the catechumens. Recording and sharing particularly meaningful input or stories can serve as a testimony to the individual's faith as well as to the power of the Spirit working in and through your parish RCIA.

The bishop ordinarily admits catechumens and candidates to their respective rites and presides at the ceremony. Whether or not the rite of election is celebrated in your parish, encourage all team members, sponsors, and close family and friends to attend. Prepare the catechumens by reviewing the steps or rehearsing the responses ahead of time. Rehearsal or a dry run in your parish church can be especially useful for children participating in these rites as it familiarizes them with what to expect on the day of the rite and helps soothe nerves or fears.

1. The rite, held within a Mass, begins with the Liturgy of the Word.

2. After the homily, the celebrant calls the catechumens forward by name, along with their godparents.

3. He addresses the assembly and asks the godparents if these young men and women are "worthy to be admitted" (*RCIA* 131). He asks if they have "sufficiently prepared… faithfully listened to God's word…[and] responded." The godparents answer, "They have."

4. He asks the catechumens if they wish to enter the Church. They answer, "We do."

5. After their names are signed in the *Book of the Elect*, the celebrant declares that they are members of the elect. He exhorts them to remain faithful and "to reach the fullness of truth" and their godparents to continue their "loving care and example" (*RCIA* 133).

6. The community offers intercessions for the elect.

7. The celebrant prays over the elect and dismisses them before continuing with the Liturgy of the Eucharist.

Sponsors and Godparents: Knowing and Making the Difference

The work of the parish (RCIA) sponsor usually begins during the period of inquiry and continues through the catechumenate. Since the official role ends with the beginning of Lent, the catechumen will choose a godparent for baptism. The godparent might be from outside the parish. He or she is ideally someone who has been and will continue to be a Christian model and support for the catechumen through life. It's the godparent's role to present the catechumen at the rite of election and to accompany him or her through the final, intense preparation for initiation. The godparent will also stand with the elect at the celebration of the sacraments and help with his or her continuing Christian formation after Easter. While many parish sponsors serve as godparents, or confirmation sponsors if their candidates are already baptized, all sponsors can continue to offer prayer and support throughout the initiation process and beyond.

Like the sponsor, a godparent must be an active Catholic. Anyone with a preexisting acquaintance is favorable, but the godparent should not be a close relative. Godparents should be able to judge the catechumen's progress and faith objectively and challenge him or her in Christian living. This responsibility may interfere with the personal support that naturally comes from family, and not all loved ones feel qualified or prepared. Candidates with eligible baptismal godparents may call on them to be confirmation sponsors. Once a godparent is chosen and approved, invite him or her to the weekly sessions and any preparations for the rites.

Both sponsors and godparents are companions who travel with their participant, represent the Catholic Church, and witness to his or her deepening relationship with Christ. Not everyone travels the same distance or at the same pace, but all learn from each other along the way. The personal connections made within and through these relationships form and unite the parish and larger Christian community. Encourage them to enjoy the journey.

Effective Catechesis During the Catechumenate

The goal of catechesis in the RCIA is conversion rather than academic or religious mastery. It should be clear, direct, and presented at the participants' level. It must be accurate, age-appropriate, and promote understanding and acceptance. It must touch their hearts and shine the light of faith on their lives. It must connect to their personal experiences or risk being discarded as irrelevant.

The catechetical model or process of faith formation generally involves three things:

1. *Life experience.*

2. *Message or doctrine.*

3. *Response.*

Personal witness is important in most, if not all, groups that discuss topics of faith, especially the RCIA. As catechists, sponsors, and participants share their stories, they begin to shape a small faith community. They better understand each other's questions, support the personal journeys of others, and reflect on their own.

The sacraments are central to the Christian life and therefore to the *Journey of Faith* catechumenate sessions as well. The images and symbols associated with each sacrament convey scriptural and theological meaning and directly relate to what we do as Catholics. Knowing this is essential to understanding and accepting our faith and will deepen the sacramental and liturgical experiences of all.

The best RCIA program goes beyond the weekly sessions to include attendance at Mass; private prayer; spiritual reading or study; and acts of charity, justice, or mercy. The process increasingly involves the community of faith, family, and others. As you approach the Easter Vigil, seek out ways in which catechumens and candidates can apply the topics, concepts, and witness to their growing faith in both word and action.

Practical Suggestions

- Once participants begin attending Mass or celebrating the word, establish signals and routines that reinforce religious devotion. Sponsors can assist you in modeling proper behaviors until participants have internalized them.

- Make the best use of your materials and resources. Learn the strengths and weaknesses of various formats, media, and types of presentations. Study the *Journey of Faith* content for prayer and activity suggestions. Know when and how to supplement, both to individuals and to all participants.

- Learn your catechumens' and candidates' needs and preferences. Continue to leave time for questions and concerns. Adjust the environment and sessions to engage many types of learners and increase understanding. Simple things like prayers, decorations, and refreshments can add interest and a personal touch.

- Connect with spiritual directors in your area who have a background working with children. Encourage their services for all participants and make them readily available.

- When presenting the sacraments, allow the catechumens to explore, and interact with them. Share photos and videos of recent ceremonies. Invite sponsors, clergy, and others to describe their experiences. Compare them to traditions and symbols in other cultures. Encourage members of your parish youth group to get involved by giving talks, making care packages, or otherwise mentoring the children in your group.

- Bring salvation and Church history to life. Show a scene from a modern rendition of an event in the Bible or the life of a saint. Share an article, press release, or stream a video from a Catholic news source on a current event or relevant topic.

Integrating the Parish Community

For many in the parish, the rites of acceptance and welcoming are a first glimpse into the RCIA process and at the new participants. This increased visibility is a prime opportunity to begin or renew the community's involvement. As the RCIA team and participants develop a rapport and feel more comfortable with the process, continue to seek out ways in which they can interact with their family in faith.

- Ensure that the pastor formally dismisses the RCIA group during Mass from the rite of acceptance until the Easter Vigil. Publicly acknowledging the catechumens' and candidates' presence affirms their dedication and heightens the community's awareness of and appreciation for this ministry. The priest's blessing also strengthens their faith and study.

- During Advent, attend a seasonal prayer service, devotion, or adoration together to expose participants to Catholic traditions.

- Remind parishioners to pray for the catechumens and candidates, to introduce themselves before or after Mass, and to share their faith with others.

- Invite parishioners to attend the weekly sessions and RCIA rites. This better reflects the communal nature of the process and demonstrates the Church's ongoing support.

- Involve team members, sponsors, and ministry members in acquiring supplies, religious objects, and audio and visual aides. Often people have these things already, eliminating the need for any purchases.

- Invite parish ministers and volunteers to speak to the participants, especially if their role or group hasn't been introduced:

  o The liturgy committee, music director, sacristans, or wedding coordinator might share how they prepare for Mass, sacraments, and funerals.

  o A Bible study or youth group might provide some information or resources on key Bible passages or events in Church history.

  o The prolife team or St. Vincent de Paul society might give examples of how they are defending human dignity and life and working for justice in the local community. They could also invite participants to contribute or volunteer.

Catechism: 1229–33, 1247–49

Objectives

- Distinguish between the rites in the RCIA for catechumens and those for baptized candidates.
- Distinguish between required and optional rites.
- Discover each rite results in a greater commitment to and unity with the greater Church.

Leader Meditation

John 1:35–42

Like the prophets before him, John the Baptist pointed the way to God and prepared individuals to hear and respond to the invitation to come and follow. While paths and intentions vary from person to person, we can shine light on Christ, the one who reveals who we are and gathers and unites us in his name.

Leader Preparation

- Read the lesson, this lesson plan, the Scripture passage, and the *Catechism* sections.
- If you haven't already, determine each child's sacramental status and formation level. Be prepared to explain the differences as the children relate to the process; refer to this guide, parish or diocesan policies, or the rites themselves.
- Gather any necessary instructions on your parish's rites of acceptance and welcoming, photos and videos of past RCIA rites, and/or schedule a former RCIA participant or parish pastor to share their experiences of the season.
- Make a list of all important dates and major events that the children will be expected to attend. Make two copies for each participant.
- Be familiar with the following vocabulary terms: commit, rite of acceptance, sacraments of initiation, rite of welcoming, rite of election, *Book of the Elect*, elect, scrutinies, Creed, Nicene Creed, rite of initiation, neophyte. The definitions are in this guide's glossary.

Welcome

Greet the children as they arrive. Check for supplies and immediate needs. Solicit questions or comments about the previous session and/or share new information and findings. Begin promptly.

Opening Scripture

John 1:35–42

Light the candle and read the passage aloud. Remind the children this is an account of Jesus calling his first disciples and that Jesus calls each of us, too. Allow for a moment of silence, then welcome any reactions.

> The mystery of Christ is so unfathomably rich that it cannot be exhausted by its expression in any single liturgical tradition. The history of the blossoming and development of these rites witnesses to a remarkable complementarity.
>
> *CCC 1201*

The RCIA Process and Rites

Lisa and Tanya were very excited to go to their next RCIA meeting.

"I feel like I belong to a special club," said Tanya.

Lisa nodded. "I don't want to miss any meetings. I really like learning all about God and faith and the Church."

"Me, too! I can't wait to be a member of the Church. I'm really glad my mom made me start coming to these meetings."

CCC 1229–33, 1247–49

The RCIA Process and Rites

As a group, come up with a class definition of what it means to "commit." Then create a list of things a person needs to do to be "committed" to something.

Some possible responses include: to be determined to do something, to be willing to give up other things for the sake of your commitment, to work hard to complete something.

Give children a chance to respond to the reflection questions on their own, then ask volunteers to share their responses to one or both of the questions.

Rite of Acceptance or Rite of Welcoming

After reading about the rite, ask the children to raise their hands if they will be participating in each rite. If they don't know, double check. Emphasize baptism as the reason for the separation between rites.

Rite of Election

Emphasize to the children that "election" in this case means saying "yes" or agreeing to something. No one will be voting to elect them into the Church, they elect, or choose to become a member of it on their own.

Give the children time to answer the reflection question on their own. Or ask each child to write a word that sums up how they feel about becoming Catholic (*nervous, scared, excited, joyful, anxious*) on an index card. The cards should remain anonymous. Collect the cards, shuffle them, and then share the words with the whole group. Chances are, a lot of participants will be feeling the same way!

When you **commit** to something, you promise to stick with it no matter what. That takes a lot of determination and perseverance. That means committing isn't always easy. Sometimes our commitment means we can do the things our friends are doing. Sometimes our commitment isn't fun all the time.

Like when you commit to getting an "A" in a class. You have to give up time with your friends to do your homework and study. You have to work really hard in class. Getting the "A" feels good. Working toward the "A" is hard.

Becoming a Catholic is like that, too. You've decided being Catholic is something you want to do. You're excited about it. You want to learn even more about the Catholic faith. But that won't always be easy. You have to attend every session. You have to talk in discussions. You have to do work and complete activities. Becoming Catholic can be hard work. But it's worth it!

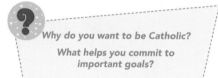

Why do you want to be Catholic?

What helps you commit to important goals?

Rites, Rites, and More Rites!

Rite of Acceptance or Rite of Welcoming

If you have never been baptized, your journey to becoming Catholic starts with the **rite of acceptance**. People in your parish will hear about how you want to be Catholic. Then, at the Easter Vigil, you will receive the three **sacraments of initiation**: baptism, confirmation, and Eucharist.

If you have already been baptized in a Christian church, your journey starts with the **rite of welcoming**. Your parish will hear about how you want to be Catholic. Then you receive the sacraments of confirmation and Eucharist.

Here is what will happen:

1. The priest will introduce each person by name and ask what he or she wants from the Church.

2. The priest will make the Sign of the Cross on each person's forehead.

3. Catechumens and candidates will stay in the church for the readings and then leave with their teachers or catechists for their own lesson.

Which rite will you be a part of?

Rite of Election

You'll keep learning about the Catholic faith. Then you'll be asked again if you want to be Catholic. This is called the **rite of election**. The rite of election usually happens on the first Sunday of Lent. In this election, the whole parish elects, or agrees, that you're ready to be Catholic.

Here is what will happen:

1. Your sponsor will talk about you and tell the Church you're ready to be Catholic.

2. The priest or bishop will ask you if you're ready to be Catholic. If you say "yes," your name is written in a special book. This book is called the ***Book of the Elect.***

3. The priest or bishop announces that you, and anyone else becoming Catholic with you, are now "members of the **elect**."

4. The rite will end with prayers and a blessing.

How do you feel about becoming Catholic (nervous, excited, scared...)? Why?

Scrutinies
(for those who've not been baptized)

When you scrutinize something, you examine it very carefully. During the **scrutinies**, you will be asked questions that help you think very carefully about yourself and your friendship with God. You will examine times where you did bad things and hurt God. Then you'll be able to say you're sorry for those things and promise to try and do better. You'll also thank God for all the good things that bring you closer to God. Finally, the priest will pray that you'll be freed from all sins.

Only those who haven't been baptized yet will get to be part of the official scrutinies. But we can always scrutinize our lives and look for ways to grow closer to God!

What's one way you can grow closer to God this week?

Presentation of the Creed

The **Creed** is the summary of major Catholic beliefs. The Creed we say at Mass is called the **Nicene Creed**, and on one of the Sundays during Lent, you will receive a copy of the Creed. This is a very important prayer for Catholics, so it's a good thing to memorize!

Presentation of the Lord's Prayer

The Lord's Prayer is also known as the Our Father. We say the Our Father during Mass (and a lot of other times!). On a Sunday during Lent, you'll receive a copy of the Lord's Prayer. Please learn this prayer by heart, too.

The Big Day

The **rite of initiation** is held on the night before Easter Sunday, called the Easter Vigil. It's a very special night. The church is in total darkness when Mass starts and then slowly lights up. This Mass is when you'll receive the sacraments for the first time. You will then be a **neophyte**, or new Catholic. The Easter Vigil is a very happy Mass because the Church is celebrating Jesus' resurrection and your new life as a Catholic!

Here is what will happen:

1. A fire is lit, and that fire lights the large paschal (Easter) candle. As the candle is carried down the aisle, people light smaller candles with its flame.

2. Special hymns are sung. Bells ring out to announce that Jesus is risen.

3. After the Gospel, where we hear about Jesus' resurrection, the priest gives a homily. Then he will call forward those who will be baptized.

4. The priest blesses the water for baptism, then pours it over each catechumen's head.

5. Those just baptized wear a white garment to show that they are a new creation.

6. They will also receive baptismal candles, lit from the paschal candle.

7. Then the candidates will be called to join the newly baptized.

8. Catechumens and candidates will say aloud that they believe in the Catholic Church.

9. They all receive the sacrament of confirmation.

10. Then the newest Catholics lead the parish in going to Communion and take part in their first Eucharist!

Scrutinies

Discuss this section with the group and remind baptized participants that even though they will not participate in the official scrutinies, they will need to examine their lives carefully, too. Encourage participants to participate in the sacrament of reconciliation (if they can).

Answer the reflection question as a group by making a list of all the ways your class can grow closer to God this week.

The Big Day

Go over the steps with your group, but remind the children they won't have to memorize the whole thing right away. The whole catechumenate period will prepare them to receive the sacraments. When the Easter Vigil arrives, they'll be prepared.

Final Activity

Give the children time to complete the activity before the end of the session. Walk around as children work and affirm correct answers and clarify any confusion. Answers are below.

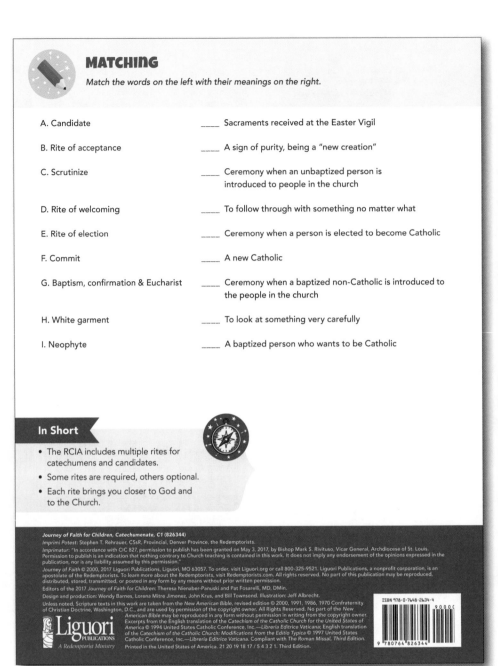

MATCHING

Match the words on the left with their meanings on the right.

A. Candidate

B. Rite of acceptance

C. Scrutinize

D. Rite of welcoming

E. Rite of election

F. Commit

G. Baptism, confirmation & Eucharist

H. White garment

I. Neophyte

_____ Sacraments received at the Easter Vigil

_____ A sign of purity, being a "new creation"

_____ Ceremony when an unbaptized person is introduced to people in the church

_____ To follow through with something no matter what

_____ Ceremony when a person is elected to become Catholic

_____ A new Catholic

_____ Ceremony when a baptized non-Catholic is introduced to the people in the church

_____ To look at something very carefully

_____ A baptized person who wants to be Catholic

In Short

- The RCIA includes multiple rites for catechumens and candidates.
- Some rites are required, others optional.
- Each rite brings you closer to God and to the Church.

Journey of Faith for Children, Catechumenate, C1 (826344)
Imprimi Potest: Stephen T. Rehrauer, CSsR, Provincial, Denver Province, the Redemptorists.
Imprimatur: "In accordance with CIC 827, permission to publish has been granted on May 3, 2017, by Bishop Mark S. Rivituso, Vicar General, Archdiocese of St. Louis. Permission to publish is an indication that nothing contrary to Church teaching is contained in this work. It does not imply any endorsement of the opinions expressed in the publication, nor is any liability assumed by this permission."
Journey of Faith © 2000, 2017 Liguori Publications, Liguori, MO 63057. To order, visit Liguori.org or call 800-325-9521. Liguori Publications, a nonprofit corporation, is an apostolate of the Redemptorists. To learn more about the Redemptorists, visit Redemptorists.com. All rights reserved. No part of this publication may be reproduced, distributed, stored, transmitted, or posted in any form by any means without prior written permission.
Editors of the 2017 *Journey of Faith for Children:* Theresa Nienaber-Panuski and Pat Fosarelli, MD, DMin.
Design and production: Wendy Barnes, Lorena Mitre Jimenez, John Krus, and Bill Townsend. Illustration: Jeff Albrecht.
Unless noted, Scripture texts in this work are taken from the *New American Bible,* revised edition © 2000, 1991, 1986, 1970 Confraternity of Christian Doctrine, Washington, D.C., and are used by permission of the copyright owner. All Rights Reserved. No part of the *New American Bible* may be reproduced in any form without permission in writing from the copyright owner. Excerpts from the English translation of the *Catechism of the Catholic Church for the United States of America* © 1994 United States Catholic Conference, Inc.—*Libreria Editrice Vaticana;* English translation of the *Catechism of the Catholic Church: Modifications from the Editio Typica* © 1997 United States Catholic Conference, Inc.—*Libreria Editrice Vaticana.* Compliant with *The Roman Missal, Third Edition.*
Printed in the United States of America. 21 20 19 18 17 / 5 4 3 2 1. Third Edition.

ISBN 978-0-7648-2634-4
9 780764 826344

A. Candidate

B. Rite of acceptance

C. Scrutinize

D. Rite of welcoming

E. Rite of election

F. Commit

G. Baptism, confirmation & Eucharist

H. White garment

I. Neophyte

__G__ Sacraments received at the Easter Vigil

__H__ A sign of purity, being a "new creation"

__B__ Ceremony when an unbaptized person is introduced to people in the church.

__F__ To follow through with something no matter what

__E__ Ceremony when a person is elected to become Catholic

__I__ A new Catholic

__D__ Ceremony when a baptized non-Catholic is introduced to the people in the church

__C__ To look at something very carefully

__A__ A baptized person who wants to be Catholic

Closing Prayer

Pray an Our Father in unison. This familiar prayer proclaims oneness in God, faithfulness to his will, and frequent nourishment as he leads us along the path of faith.

Take-Home

Provide the children with two copies of a list of important dates and major events of the RCIA process. Ask them to provide this list to their sponsor or godparents and parents. Encourage them to put these dates on their calendar or their family calendar before the next lesson.

C2: The Sacraments: An Introduction

Catechism: 1084, 1087, 113–34, 1210–12, 1420–21, 1533–35

Objectives

- List the seven official sacraments of the Church.
- Discover the sacraments have their roots in Jesus' teaching and the New Testament.
- Define the sacraments as tangible signs of God's love.

Leader Meditation

Matthew 28:16–20

Jesus promises, "I am with you always, to the end of the age." Through the sacraments, there are visible signs of the Lord's presence in the Church and in our lives. Each sacrament we receive not only increases the Lord's presence but also increases our own awareness of that presence. We don't walk our journey of faith alone. Jesus walks with us every step of the way.

Leader Preparation

- Read the lesson, this lesson plan, the Scripture passage, and the *Catechism* sections. Be prepared to respond to concerns surrounding sacramental doctrine and practice.
- Doing something special for your class this week or inviting the parish outreach or hospitality team to do so would fit with this lesson's message. Candy or other inexpensive gifts would demonstrate that outward signs express invisible realities—like the parish's ongoing support.
- Be familiar with this vocabulary term: sacrament. The definition is in this guide's glossary.

Welcome

Greet the children as they arrive. Check for supplies and immediate needs. Solicit questions or comments about the previous lesson and/or share new information and findings. Begin promptly.

Opening Scripture

Matthew 28:16–20

Light the candle and read aloud. Following the reading, ask the children to list the ways Jesus is "with us always."

> Sacraments are "powers that come forth" from the Body of Christ, which is ever-living and life-giving. They are actions of the Holy Spirit at work in his Body, the Church. *CCC 1116*

The Sacraments: An Introduction

"Today we're going to talk about love," Mrs. Evans announced.

Terrence and Tomás looked at each and rolled their eyes. Tomás said, "What does love have to do with being Catholic? I didn't think we had to be in love to be Catholic!"

Mrs. Evans smiled. "Not romantic love. Today we're going to talk about God's love. God loves all of us very much. So much that he even died for us."

CCC 1084, 1087, 113–34, 1210–12, 1420–21, 1533–35

The Sacraments: An Introduction

Create a Venn diagram on the board (if you have one) and list traits of romantic love and family love.

Romantic love: you think the other person is cute (attraction), you have a crush on someone, you give that person gifts, you write special letters, you're always thinking about them, and so on.

Family love: you want what's best for each other, you don't always get along, you take care of each other, you cheer each other up, and so on.

Ways to Say, "I Love You"

Ask the children to respond to the reflection question on their own.

As a group, come up with some other examples of ways you can say, "I love you" to the people you care about.

You tell God, "I love you" by paying attention during Mass or praying on your own. You can tell your grandparents, "I love you" by doing yard work for them without being asked. You can tell out-of-town family, "I love you" by sending them a card or giving them a call for no reason.

How does God show he loves you?

How did Jesus say, "I love you"?

Ways to Say, "I Love You"

Your grandmother is coming to visit. You haven't seen her in a long time. When you greet her at the door, how will you say, "I love you, Grandma"?

You can say, "I love you" with a hug.

Your best friend is sick in bed. You miss him very much. You know he misses you, too. How will you say, "I love you" to your best friend?

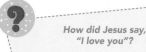

You can say, "I love you" with a card or visit.

It's your mom's birthday. You want to give her something, but you have no money. How will you say, "I love you, Mom"?

You can say, "I love you" by helping her around the house.

Your father comes home very tired. You want to show him love and comfort. How will you say, "I love you"?

Best of all, you can just say, "I love you, Dad."

How Does Jesus Say, "I Love You"?

Jesus said, "I love you" to people in many ways. We can read about Jesus' love in the Bible.

Jesus Cures the Leper

One day, Jesus was walking with a crowd of people. A man with leprosy asked him, "Lord, if you choose, you can make me clean." Jesus touched him, saying, "I do choose. Be made clean!" Right away, the man was cured.

Adapted from Matthew 8:1–3

Jesus Feeds the Crowd

Jesus was speaking to a crowd of 5,000 people. It was late, and the people were hungry. The disciples said, "Send them away so they can get something to eat." But Jesus said, "Feed them yourselves." They had only two fish and five loaves of bread, not enough to feed everyone. Jesus then said, "Ask them to sit in groups of fifty." Jesus looked up to heaven and blessed and broke the food. The disciples took the pieces of fish and bread and fed all the people. And there was some left over.

Adapted from Luke 9:12–17

How did Jesus say, "I love you"?

How Does Jesus Say, "I Love You"?

You can go over each of the following sections as a group or, if you want a more interactive session, split children up into four groups and have each group cover a Scripture passage to share with the rest of the group. If you need more groups, you can use the additional stories at the end of the section: John 9:6–7 and Luke 19:1–10.

Jesus Cures the Leper

Jesus says, "I love you" by curing the man with leprosy because the man had great faith in Jesus.

Jesus Feeds the Crowd

Jesus says, "I love you" by feeding the people abundantly (more food than they needed).

Jesus Serves His Friends

At the Last Supper, Jesus got up from the table, took off his robe, and tied a towel around his waist. Then he washed his disciples' feet and wiped them clean with the towel. Jesus said, "I have set an example for you. You are to serve others just as I have served you."

Adapted from John 13:4–15

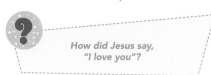

How did Jesus say, "I love you"?

Jesus Cares for Children

People were bringing their babies and children to Jesus so that he could bless them, but his disciples tried to make them stay away. Jesus became angry and said, "Let the children come to me and do not stop them, because the kingdom of heaven belongs to them." Then he blessed and hugged the children.

Adapted from Mark 10:13–16

How did Jesus say, "I love you"?

There are many other Bible stories about how Jesus said, "I love you" while he was in this world. Jesus touched, fed, cured, and helped people. Look up the following stories in the Bible and see what a loving teacher Jesus is. What did he do in each story?

- John 9:6–7
- Luke 19:1–10

Jesus Still Says, "I Love You"

Jesus promised his disciples that he would be with them always. Jesus is with us today in the sacraments. A **sacrament** is a visible sign of something that's real but can't be seen. When the priest pours water on someone during baptism, it's a sign that God is *really* washing away that person's sin. The seven sacraments of the Church are Jesus' way of touching, feeding, and healing us today.

All the sacraments began with something Jesus did or said. The words, things, and symbols are not magic or pretending. Through each sacrament, Jesus *really* comes to us and cares for us in the world.

Write down three ways you can say or show love like Jesus did.

1. _____

_____

2. _____

_____

3. _____

_____

Jesus Serves His Friends

Jesus says, "I love you" by washing his friends' feet to show them how much he cared for them, and to show them how to serve others.

Jesus Cares for Children

Jesus says, "I love you" by not turning away the children and by giving the children blessings.

After reading each of the next two Scripture passages, answer "How did Jesus say, 'I love you?'" as a group.

- **John 9:6–7**
  Jesus says, "I love you" by giving the blind man his sight back.
- **Luke 19:1–10**
  Jesus says, "I love you" by showing mercy and forgiveness to Zacchaeus, even though Zacchaeus had done bad things in the past, because Zacchaeus was truly sorry for his actions.

Jesus Still Says, "I Love You"

Give the children time to respond to the reflection question on their own. Then ask each child to give one of the ways she or he can show love to Jesus, and collect responses on a class list. You can even turn this class list into a "Ways We Love Jesus" poster to hang up in your classroom or in the entry to your parish church to get parishioners involved in your RCIA classes.

Final Activity

Give the children time to complete the activity in class. Answers are below.

Seek and Find

The following words are hidden somewhere in the jumble. Can you find them all?

FEEDING
HEALING
LOVE
PRESENCE
SACRAMENT
SIGN
TOUCHING

```
G  B  M  S  V  H  I  D  F  S  T  C  F  S  N
J  O  J  Z  F  E  O  W  W  E  N  K  S  O  S
I  Q  Z  B  O  A  L  J  S  P  E  I  U  N  E
D  F  C  S  G  L  O  E  C  E  M  D  Y  H  Y
T  P  I  L  A  I  C  G  D  J  A  Y  I  P  V
L  G  S  V  E  N  E  V  O  L  R  O  U  N  G
N  X  I  W  E  G  B  T  O  U  C  H  I  N  G
O  P  Q  S  H  P  O  V  S  Q  A  X  T  L  A
F  X  E  F  M  T  T  N  G  K  S  Z  J  I  W
Y  R  W  X  A  C  Q  E  V  C  U  K  A  U  V
P  E  P  T  E  U  A  T  L  F  C  V  U  Y  V
```

In Short

- The Church has seven official sacraments.
- Jesus started the sacraments on earth.
- Sacraments are physical signs of God's love.

Journey of Faith for Children, Catechumenate, C2 (826344)

Imprimi Potest: Stephen T. Rehrauer, CSsR, Provincial, Denver Province, the Redemptorists.

Imprimatur: "In accordance with CIC 827, permission to publish has been granted on May 3, 2017, by Bishop Mark S. Rivituso, Vicar General, Archdiocese of St. Louis. Permission to publish is an indication that nothing contrary to Church teaching is contained in this work. It does not imply any endorsement of the opinions expressed in the publication, nor is any liability assumed by this permission."

Journey of Faith © 2000, 2017 Liguori Publications, Liguori, MO 63057. To order, visit Liguori.org or call 800-325-9521. Liguori Publications, a nonprofit corporation, is an apostolate of the Redemptorists. To learn more about the Redemptorists, visit Redemptorists.com. All rights reserved. No part of this publication may be reproduced, distributed, stored, transmitted, or posted in any form by any means without prior written permission.

Editors of the 2017 *Journey of Faith for Children:* Theresa Nienaber-Panuski and Pat Fosarelli, MD, DMin.

Design and production: Wendy Barnes, Lorena Mitre Jimenez, John Krus, and Bill Townsend. Illustration: Jeff Albrecht.

Unless noted, Scripture texts in this work are taken from the *New American Bible*, revised edition © 2010, 1991, 1986, 1970 Confraternity of Christian Doctrine, Washington, D.C., and are used by permission of the copyright owner. All Rights Reserved. No part of the *New American Bible* may be reproduced in any form without permission in writing from the copyright owner. Excerpts from the English translation of the *Catechism of the Catholic Church for the United States of America* © 1994 United States Catholic Conference, Inc.—*Libreria Editrice Vaticana*; English translation of the *Catechism of the Catholic Church: Modifications from the Editio Typica* © 1997 United States Catholic Conference, Inc.—*Libreria Editrice Vaticana*. Compliant with *The Roman Missal, Third Edition*.

Printed in the United States of America. 21 20 19 18 17 / 5 4 3 2 1. Third Edition.

Liguori
PUBLICATIONS
A Redemptorist Ministry

```
G  B  M  S  V  H  I  D  F  S  T  C  F  S  N
J  O  J  Z  F  E  O  W  W  E  N  K  S  O  S
I  Q  Z  B  O  A  L  J  S  P  E  I  U  N  E
D  F  C  S  G  L  O  E  C  E  M  D  Y  H  Y
T  P  I  L  A  I  C  G  D  J  A  Y  I  P  V
L  G  S  V  E  N  E  V  O  L  R  O  U  N  G
N  X  I  W  E  G  B  T  O  U  C  H  I  N  G
O  P  Q  S  H  P  O  V  S  Q  A  X  T  L  A
F  X  E  F  M  T  T  N  G  K  S  Z  J  I  W
Y  R  W  X  A  C  Q  E  V  C  U  K  A  U  V
P  E  P  T  E  U  A  T  L  F  C  V  U  Y  V
```

Closing Prayer

Pray the Glory Be as a group. This simple prayer proclaims God's faithful presence in our lives— yesterday, today, and tomorrow.

Take-Home

Ask the children to pick one member of their family (in their head, they don't have to say the name aloud) to show their love this week with words or actions.

Catechism: 1213–84

Objectives

- Recognize baptism is one of the seven sacraments of the Church.
- Begin to discover the historical and scriptural roots of baptism.
- List some of the significant symbols of baptism.

Leader Meditation

Mark 1:4–11

Most of us can't recall our own baptisms. Yet many times along our journey, we review and remake the promises made for us by our godparents. In preparation for this lesson, renew your baptismal promises and pray for the grace and strength to become all that God has created you to become.

Leader Preparation

- Read the lesson, this lesson plan, the Scripture passage, and the *Catechism* sections.
- Have a copy of the baptismal promises to reflect upon for a closing prayer.
- Bring in holy water, oil of chrism, a white baptismal gown, and a baptismal candle to pass around.
- Be familiar with the following vocabulary terms: water, oil of chrism, white garment, candle. The definitions are in this guide's glossary.

Welcome

Greet the children as they arrive. Check for supplies and immediate needs. Solicit questions or comments about the previous session and/or share new information and findings. Begin promptly.

Opening Scripture

Mark 1:4–11

Light the candle and read aloud. Before beginning the session handout, create a list of all the elements present at Jesus' baptism: Someone to perform the baptism (John), water, God the Father, the Holy Spirit, a dove, and other people.

> The faith required for Baptism is not a perfect and mature faith, but a beginning that is called to develop. The catechumen or the godparent is asked: "What do you ask of God's Church?" The response is: "Faith."
>
> CCC 1253

The Sacrament of Baptism

"Why can't people be baptized without getting all wet?" Tanya whispered to Terrence.

Mrs. Evans overheard them. "That's a great question!" she said. "Water is an important sign of baptism. What do you think water could be a sign of?"

CCC 1213–84

CHILDREN

The Sacrament of Baptism

Answer the discussion question as a group. If the children have trouble coming up with an answer, ask them to think about Jesus' baptism in the Scripture passage you just read or some of the uses of water.

Water helps us keep clean, water helps us wash things, drinking water keeps us healthy, and so on. In baptism, water cleanses us (makes us clean) and washes away our original sin. Baptism gives us the grace to live a spiritually healthy life.

John the Baptist: Chosen By God

As you read through this section, ask the children who they think will take the role of John the Baptist during their baptism? *(The priest.)* And why? *(The priest has been given [ordained to do] a special job by God. The priest tells us about Jesus and what God wants for our lives. Through the priest, God gives us grace and washes away our sins.)*

Joining the Family of God

After you read this section, if you have time, create a list of "God's Family Rules" as a group. You can start this activity by asking the children if they've heard of the Ten Commandments or the Golden Rule. This can be your starting place. Emphasize to the children that, just like in our own families, the rules aren't there to make our lives miserable but to keep us safe and happy.

Some of your family rules might include helping others, not gossiping or talking mean about others, doing chores without being asked or without getting an allowance, obeying our parents the first time they ask us to do something, being respectful of other people's things, and using appropriate language even when we're upset.

? *Why do you think water is so important for baptism?*

John the Baptist: Chosen by God

John the Baptist was unusual. He wore clothes made of camel's hair. He ate grasshoppers and honey. He lived alone in the wilderness far from villages and towns. People from miles around came to hear John speak. He told the people to turn to God and begin living a new life. Then he baptized them in the waters of the Jordan River. That is why he was called John "the Baptist." Baptizing people with water symbolized that their sins were washed away.

God chose John for another job that was even more important. John was to tell everyone that Jesus was coming. John said,

> "I am baptizing you with water, for repentance, but the one who is coming after me is mightier than I" *(Matthew 3:11; see also Luke 3:16 and Mark 1:7–8).*

Jesus is "the one" who is more powerful than John, and today Jesus baptizes every new Christian with the Holy Spirit.

Beginning Your New Life

The first sacrament you receive when you become a Catholic is baptism. When you are baptized, you are reborn into the family of Jesus. In your new life, Jesus leads and guides you in his way of love. In your new life, you live for God, just like Jesus did when he was in the world.

Joining the Family of God

You belong to God's family the moment you're baptized. This family is all the people who pray with you in church and who pray to Jesus across the world. That's a very big family!

Just like your family at home, being a member of God's family comes with responsibilities. At home you have to do chores, help around the house, and obey your parents' rules. It's the same in God's family. You have to serve others, help those in need, and obey God's commandments.

What Happens at a Baptism?

When you're baptized, the priest or deacon will pour water on your head or guide your head into the baptismal font or pool. **Water** is a sign that all your sins are washed away through baptism. You are a new person, fresh and clean—just like clothes coming out of the washer.

Water also makes things grow. Farmers rely on water to produce their crops. Flowers, grass, and trees couldn't live without water—neither could animals or people. When you're baptized, the holy water helps you grow in love and in your new life with God.

What Happens at a Baptism?

As you go over each step of the sacrament, pass around the related symbol so children can see and touch it. This is helpful even for children who have already been baptized because not all Christian churches use all the same baptismal symbols.

You may also ask children who have been baptized to share if their baptism included any of these symbols, too. Emphasize the shared symbols and the unity all Christian churches share in the sacrament of baptism, which is why those previously baptized will not receive the sacrament again.

After your baptism, you are anointed with the **oil of chrism**. This is a special oil blessed by a bishop. This anointing signifies that you belong to the kingdom of God.

Next, you're clothed in a white robe or **white garment**, which shows that you're a new person and that you have wrapped yourself in Jesus.

Now What?

As a new Catholic, you will:

- Learn about Jesus and God's love for us by reading the Bible, participating in weekly Mass, and going to religious-education classes.

- Follow the Ten Commandments, the laws God gave to his people many hundreds of years ago.

- Receive the sacraments that Jesus gave to his Church.

- Love others as Jesus has loved you.

- Best of all, live in the peace and happiness of God's family!

Finally, your parent or godparent will light a **candle** from the big paschal candle, symbolizing that we share in Christ's death and resurrection. Also, we say that Jesus is the Light of the World. Your baptismal candle shows that Jesus is your light, too. You are now called a "child of the light."

Now What?

Ask the children what they're looking forward to about being baptized and a member of the Catholic Church.

Final Activity

Give the children time at the end of the session to complete the activity. Walk around as the children work, affirming correct answers and clarifying any confusion. If the children have questions about their own baptism or sacramental status that you're unable to answer, make a note of such questions and follow up after the lesson.

Answers to the activity are provided below.

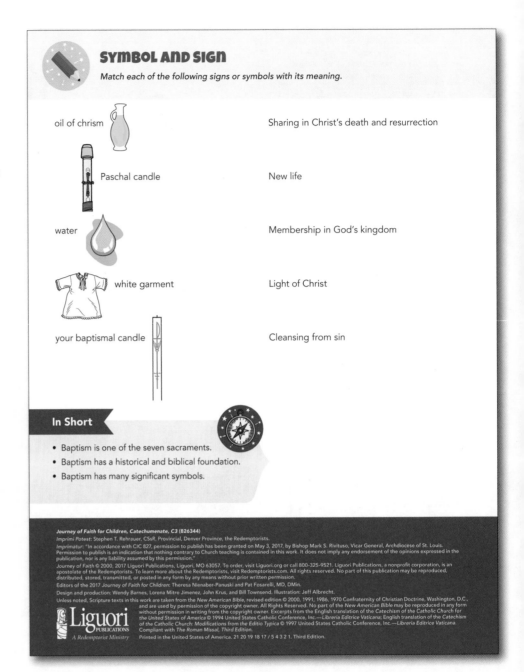

Oil of chrism	Membership in God's kingdom
Easter candle	Sharing in Christ's death and resurrection
Water	Cleansing from sin
White garment	New life
Your baptismal candle	Light of Christ

Closing Prayer

As a closing prayer, ask the
children to follow along as you
read each of the baptismal
promises aloud. End with the
following prayer. Ask the children
to repeat each line after you.

Lord Jesus Christ,
give us the grace
to fulfill our baptismal promises
each day of our lives
as we strive
to rise with you.
Thank you for this sacrament,
for washing away sin,
and for raising us up
to a life of grace.
Amen.

Take-Home

Ask the children and their parents
to create their own "God's Family
Rules" at home this week and post
them in a place where everyone
can see them.

C4: The Sacrament of Confirmation

Catechism: 1285–1321

Objectives

- Recognize that through confirmation the Spirit empowers us as disciples and witnesses.
- Consider the significance of sponsor and baptismal (saint) name.
- Identify the actions that confer the sacrament of confirmation.

Leader Meditation

Acts 1:8–11 and Acts 8:14–17

We have all been witnesses to the fulfillment of Jesus' promise to send the Holy Spirit. This Spirit comes, also as promised, with the power to make us witnesses to the whole world. Your witness—that is, your daily love-filled, Christ-centered living—is your most effective tool in passing on the faith to the young people in your care.

Leader Preparation

- Read the lesson, this lesson plan, the Scripture passage, and the *Catechism* sections.
- If your budget allows or you can find a parish ministry to donate, get copies of *Choosing Confirmation Names for Young Women* or *Choosing Confirmation Names for Young Men* for each child in your group to help them choose a confirmation name. (Both these pamphlets are available from Liguori Publications at Liguori.org.)
- Be familiar with the following vocabulary terms: laying on of hands, anointed, sponsor. The definitions are in this guide's glossary.

Welcome

Greet the children as they arrive. Check for supplies and immediate needs. Solicit questions or comments about the previous session and/or share new information and findings. Begin promptly.

Opening Scripture

Acts 1:8–11 and Acts 8:14–17

Light the candle and read aloud. Explain that the symbolic action described in Acts 8, the laying on of hands, remains an important part of the confirmation ritual today. Before you begin your lesson, ask the children what they think it means to "receive the Spirit."

> It must be explained to the faithful that the reception of the sacrament of Confirmation is necessary for the completion of baptismal grace. For "by the sacrament of Confirmation, [the baptized] are more perfectly bound to the Church and are enriched with, a special strength of the Holy Spirit."
>
> CCC 1285

The Sacrament of Confirmation

Lisa and Tomás were staying late to help clean up the classroom. "My cousin says that once you get confirmed you don't have to go to church anymore. But that seems dumb. Why get confirmed if you're not gonna go to church?" Tomás said.

Lisa shook her head, "My aunt said when you get confirmed you get to do cool stuff in church. That it gives you more responsibility."

Tomás frowned. "So, what does getting confirmed mean?"

CCC 1285–1321

Growing Up in the Faith

Give the children time to answer the "Name three things..." question. If they need help, you can prompt them by asking if there are any new classes they can take now that they couldn't take last year, or even something as simple as reaching higher shelves than they could last year.

You can also ask if there are any things children are looking forward to doing when they have grown up even more.

Then, ask the group if there is anything they are looking forward to doing when they are grown-up in the Church. This can include ways they can help others, serving in parish ministry, or talking to others about their faith.

Give the children time to answer the question "How can you help others right now?" on their own. You can ask for volunteers to share.

What Happens at Confirmation?

As you go over the symbols of confirmation, ask for a volunteer and demonstrate the laying-on of hands so the children have a visual aid to go with the description.

Growing Up in the Faith

You first receive the Holy Spirit at your baptism, when you enter into God's family. At your confirmation, you receive the power to go out and do good things for God and to speak to others about God's love. Being confirmed is like growing up in your faith.

Growing up doesn't happen all at once. There are so many things you can do this year that you couldn't do last year. Every day you learn new things, grow, and change.

Name three things you can do this year that you couldn't do last year.

1. _____

_____

2. _____

_____

3. _____

_____

Before Jesus ascended to heaven, he promised all his disciples that they would receive power from the Holy Spirit to go out and tell the world about Jesus. Jesus kept his promise. When the disciples were all together in a room, something wonderful happened. They heard a noise like the wind all through the house. Then tongues of fire came and rested above their heads. They were filled with the Holy Spirit and began to speak about Jesus and God's love. They went out immediately and preached the good news everywhere.

Adapted from Acts 1:8

As you begin your new life in the Holy Spirit, you will learn many things. You will also become stronger and braver. At confirmation, the Holy Spirit gives you the strength and courage to face your responsibilities as God's child. You will learn to use your gifts, talents, and special abilities to help the Church in the world.

How can you help others right now?

What Happens at Confirmation?

Confirmation has two very important symbols: anointing and the laying on of hands.

The **laying on of hands** is a sign that the Holy Spirit has been invited to live in you. Remember how Jesus healed people by touching them? In the same way, you are given the gift of the Holy Spirit with a touch from the minister of the sacrament.

Then you are **anointed** with a special oil that has been blessed by the bishop. The minister of the sacrament will make the Sign of the Cross on your forehead and say, "Be sealed with the gift of the Holy Spirit." You will say "Amen." Amen means, "So be it!" "Yes!" or "Right!"

You will need to choose a **sponsor** for your confirmation. This person will help you grow as a Christian and be your spiritual friend. At confirmation, your sponsor will place his or her right hand on your right shoulder and present you to the Church and God. If you need some advice on choosing a sponsor, ask your catechist, RCIA leader, or pastor for help.

You will also be asked to choose a confirmation name to remind you of your identity as a mature Christian. You can choose the name of a saint who is special to you or even the name you were given at baptism.

Who in your life would make a good sponsor?

What name do you want to take for confirmation?

Gifts of the Spirit

The Holy Spirit will give you special gifts to help you follow Jesus. Below are some of the Holy Spirit's gifts (see Isaiah 11:2–3).

- **Wisdom:** When we're wise, we know what's true. We also know the right way to act in different situations.

- **Understanding:** When we show understanding, we see every side of a situation. We understand the other person's side of an argument.

- **Guidance (or Counsel):** When we use the gift of guidance we know how to help other people. We are able to give good, clear advice that leads other people to God.

- **Knowledge:** Kind of like being book-smart, knowledge means having the information we need to know what's going on.

- **Wonder and Awe (or Fear of the Lord):** When we use this gift, we show respect for God and all holy things. We find God wonderful and awesome!

- **Reverence (or Piety):** When we show reverence, we show respect for God and his creation, and all holy things.

Which gifts of the Spirit do you wish you had right now?

Gifts of the Holy Spirit

Emphasize that, when confirmed, children will receive the gifts of the Holy Spirit in a special way, but it's still up to them to use these gifts.

Give time for the children to respond to the reflection question on their own. Encourage them to also consider how they might use those gifts if they had them as well.

Choosing a Sponsor and Confirmation Name

As a group, create a list of traits a good confirmation sponsor should have. Be sure to include those traits that are necessary for a sponsor, such as being beyond the age of reason, a confirmed and practicing Catholic, and not an immediate family member.

Other traits might include a good listener, someone who is easy to talk to about difficult things, someone you admire from church, someone involved in the same parish ministries you're interested in, and so on.

Then, as a group, discuss choosing a confirmation name. Encourage the children to do more than just pick a name that sounds cool, and to choose a saint they feel inspired by.

Give the children time to complete the two reflection questions on their own or as a group.

If you have copies of *Choosing Confirmation Names* to distribute, do that now.

Final Activity

Give the children time to complete the final activity on their own or with a partner before the end of class. The first row has been given as an example below.

WHO HAS IT?

For each gift of the Holy Spirit, write the name of someone you know who has this gift. Then write an example of how that person uses this gift.

Gift	Who has it?	Example
Wisdom		
Understanding		
Guidance (or Counsel)		
Knowledge		
Wonder and Awe (or Fear of the Lord)		
Reverence (or Piety)		

In Short

- Confirmation makes us disciples and witnesses.
- Your choices of a sponsor and a name are important.
- Confirmation includes many actions and symbols.

Journey of Faith for Children, Catechumenate, C4 (826344)
Imprimi Potest: Stephen T. Rehrauer, CSsR, Provincial, Denver Province, the Redemptorists.
Imprimatur: "In accordance with CIC 827, permission to publish has been granted on May 3, 2017, by Bishop Mark S. Rivituso, Vicar General, Archdiocese of St. Louis. Permission to publish is an indication that nothing contrary to Church teaching is contained in this work. It does not imply any endorsement of the opinions expressed in the publication, nor is any liability assumed by this permission."
Journey of Faith © 2000, 2017 Liguori Publications, Liguori, MO 63057. To order, visit Liguori.org or call 800-325-9521. Liguori Publications, a nonprofit corporation, is an apostolate of the Redemptorists. To learn more about the Redemptorists, visit Redemptorists.com. All rights reserved. No part of this publication may be reproduced, distributed, stored, transmitted, or posted in any form by any means without prior written permission.
Editors of the 2017 Journey of Faith for Children: Theresa Nienaber-Panuski and Pat Fosarelli, MD, DMin.
Design and production: Wendy Barnes, Lorena Mitre Jimenez, John Krus, and Bill Townsend. Illustration: Jeff Albrecht.
Unless noted, Scripture texts in this work are taken from the New American Bible, revised edition © 2000, 1991, 1986, 1970 Confraternity of Christian Doctrine, Washington, D.C., and are used by permission of the copyright owner. All Rights Reserved. No part of the New American Bible may be reproduced in any form without permission in writing from the copyright owner. Excerpts from the English translation of the Catechism of the Catholic Church for the United States of America © 1994 United States Catholic Conference, Inc.—Libreria Editrice Vaticana; English translation of the Catechism of the Catholic Church: Modifications from the Editio Typica © 1997 United States Catholic Conference, Inc.—Libreria Editrice Vaticana. Compliant with The Roman Missal, Third Edition.
Printed in the United States of America. 21 20 19 18 17 / 5 4 3 2 1. Third Edition.

Liguori
PUBLICATIONS
A Redemptorist Ministry

Gift	Who has it?	Example
Wisdom	*My dad.*	*When my sister and I get into arguments, my dad's able to step in and get us to calm down. He always seems to know what the real problem is and how to help us fix it.*
Understanding		
Guidance (or Counsel)		
Courage		
Knowledge		
Wonder and Awe in God's Presence		
Reverence		

Closing Prayer

Conclude the lesson by reading this excerpt from the Prayer to the Holy Spirit (or Come, Holy Spirit) and then ask the children for any special intentions.

Lord, by the light of the Holy Spirit you have illumined the hearts of your faithful. In the same Spirit, help us to relish what is right and always rejoice in your consolation. We ask this through Christ, our Lord. Amen.

Take-Home

With their parents' help, ask the children to create a list of names of possible godparents or sponsors (if they do not already have one) and a list of possible confirmation names.

C5: The Sacrament of the Eucharist

Catechism: 1322–1419

Objectives

- Recognize the scriptural context for Catholic teaching on the Eucharist.
- Relate and reflect on the Real Presence in the Eucharist.
- Identify the call to imitate Christ, especially through sacrifice.

Leader Meditation

John 6:25–51

As Catholics, our faith in the Real Presence of our Lord in the Eucharist sets us apart from many other Christian churches. Meditate on this passage from St. John's Gospel, which proclaims the central truth upon which all Catholic truths are based. Our faith must be like that of the apostles, who answered Jesus, saying, "Master, to whom shall we go? You have the words of eternal life" (John 6:68).

Leader Preparation

- Read the lesson, this lesson plan, the Scripture passage, and the *Catechism* sections. This may help you answer questions from children coming from faith traditions that view holy Communion as only symbolic.
- If possible, try to schedule a time of eucharistic adoration for your RCIA group.
- If you can, show the children unconsecrated bread and wine, plus a Communion chalice and a paten.
- Be familiar with the following vocabulary terms: Eucharist, substance. The definitions are in this guide's glossary.

Welcome

Greet participants as they arrive. Check for supplies and immediate needs. Solicit questions or comments about the previous session and/or share new information and findings. Begin promptly.

Opening Scripture

John 6:25–51

Light the candle and read aloud. Before you begin the lesson, ask the children what they think it means when Jesus says he is the "bread of life" or "bread come down from heaven."

> The holy Eucharist completes Christian initiation. Those who have been raised to the dignity of the royal priesthood by Baptism and configured more deeply to Christ by confirmation participate with the whole community in the Lord's own sacrifice by means of the Eucharist.
>
> *CCC 1322*

The Sacrament of the Eucharist

"The Eucharist can be a complicated mystery to understand," Mrs. Evans said. "Some people believe that the bread and wine are just symbols. Or that the bread and wine don't remain the Body and Blood after Communion. As Catholics, we believe the bread and wine really become the Body and Blood of Jesus."

"But what does it taste like?" asked Tanya.

"Why didn't Jesus just make a different way of sharing himself?" wondered Terrence.

Mrs. Evans said, "Communion still tastes like bread and wine even though it's been transformed. Jesus had a reason for sharing himself in this way. We're going to read about it in Scripture."

CCC 1322–1419

The Sacrament of the Eucharist

Answer the reflection question at the top of the next page as a group by writing down questions on the board or in another place where you can keep track of them. You'll come back to these questions at the end of the lesson to see which ones you've answered and which ones you may need to check on and then answer at the next lesson.

The Last Supper of Jesus

Depending on the average age of the children in your group, you may want to read the actual Scripture passages cited in the lesson.

After you've read through the story of the Last Supper, ask the children what actions Jesus did or what symbols and words he used during the meal.

He preached to his apostles before the meal, he used bread and wine, he lifted the bread up and broke it, he called the bread his Body, he lifted up the cup (chalice), he said the wine was his Blood, he shared the meal with his friends, and so on.

Once you've gone through the story, ask children if these actions, words, or symbols remind them of anything. *(They should think of the Mass.)*

Then ask the children what happened after the Last Supper. *(Jesus sacrificed himself on the cross for our sins.)* Emphasize to the children the importance of Jesus really and truly offering himself up on the cross for our sins. Not only did Jesus give us his Body and Blood at the Last Supper, he also gave up his body and shed his blood for us on the cross.

Ask the children to think about ways they can live like Jesus by sacrificing for others. Then ask each child to share a way, compiling all replies into a list. *(Responses will vary, but some may include sacrificing time to do extra chores at home, giving up part of an allowance to donate to the collection at Mass on Sunday, and sacrificing play time to help a younger sibling or classmate with schoolwork.)*

What questions do you have about the Eucharist?

The Last Supper of Jesus
(adapted from Matthew 26:26–29)

Jesus was at supper with his closest friends. He was sitting near Peter, James, and John. As everyone gathered at the table, Jesus talked about many things. Jesus told his friends about a love that never ends. "You are all my friends," he said.

Then he broke and shared the bread. "This is my body," Jesus said. "It will be given up so all of you may live." Then he filled a cup and said, "This is the blood I shed. My own life will be the best gift I can give."

This made his friends sad, but he told them to be happy. God had planned it this way. "I will come again, and then you all will know that the Son of God is in the world to stay."

We call this biblical event in history the Last Supper because it's the last meal Jesus shared before his crucifixion. Through the power of God and the working of the Holy Spirit we celebrate the Last Supper of Jesus at every Mass.

We call it the **Eucharist**, and it's a holy meal you get to share with Jesus and the whole Church.

Sharing a Special Meal

Sharing a meal together is a way to get to know people better and show we care. Families talk about their days over dinner. When we have friends come in from out of town we invite them over to share a meal. We celebrate holidays by getting together with relatives for a special meal.

List three times you and your family or friends share a meal. Then in one or two sentences explain why that meal is special.

1._____

_____

_____

2._____

_____

_____

3._____

_____

_____

The Real Presence of Jesus

In the sacrament of the Eucharist, you will receive the Body and Blood of Jesus—just like his disciples at the Last Supper. We know Jesus is really present in the form of bread and wine because Jesus told his disciples, "This is my body." He didn't say, "This is a symbol of my body" or, "This is both my body and blood and bread and wine." The bread and wine truly become the Body and Blood of Jesus.

Sharing a Special Meal

Give the children time to respond to the reflection question. They may need to continue their answers on a separate sheet of paper. Then ask them to find a partner and share one of their responses.

The Real Presence of Jesus

Emphasize that the Eucharist really does become the Body and Blood of Jesus even though its appearance remains the same. Remind the children that the sacraments are physical signs of invisible realities, just like the appearance of bread and wine is a physical sign of God's invisible presence.

When the priest calls on the Holy Spirit at Mass, God makes Jesus as present as the person sitting next to us in the pew. What we see and touch points us to a reality that remains invisible. When we eat his Body and drink his Blood, Jesus enters our hearts to help us live in his love.

The Eucharist still looks and tastes like bread and wine even though it's been transformed. That's because it's **substance**, what something really is, changes even though its appearance doesn't. We can't explain how this happens, but we believe because Jesus told us it's true. It's a mystery of faith. Only God holds the answer.

The Unbelievable Promise

Jesus made a special promise about the Eucharist. One day, when he was teaching a large crowd, he said, "I am the living bread that came down from heaven; whoever eats this bread will live forever… and I will raise him on the last day" (John 6:51, 54).

Many people didn't understand what Jesus was saying. "This is too hard to believe," they said, and walked away. But the disciples stayed because they believed the promise Jesus made about eternal life. They wanted to be with him forever.

Jesus makes this promise to you, too. If you eat this bread, Jesus' Body, you will live forever with God in heaven.

A Super Kind of Love

After the Last Supper, Jesus did exactly what he promised—he suffered and died on the cross for us. It must have been hard for his Mother and friends to watch his suffering. But imagine their joy when Jesus came back from the dead on Easter! That day they knew the power of Jesus' love. They knew his promise of eternal life would come true.

When we receive the Eucharist at Mass, we remember that Jesus gave his life for us. We remember that his sacrifice gives us eternal life and saves us from death. We remember and thank God for Jesus. Eucharist even means thanksgiving!

Thank you, Jesus!

A Super Kind of Love

As you discuss the Eucharist as Thanksgiving, go around the room and ask each child to share one thing she or he wants to thank Jesus for today. After each statement, the rest of the group responds, "Thank you, Jesus."

Final Activity

Give the children time at the end of the session to complete the final activity. Walk around as the children work and affirm correct answers and offer clarity on any points of confusion. The children's answers may vary. Sample responses follow for your reference.

List three things you learned about the Eucharist today.

1. It's really Jesus' Body and Blood.

2. It still tastes like bread and wine.

3. It's a meal we share with the Church.

List three promises Jesus made about the Eucharist.

1. The Eucharist is really Jesus' Body and Blood.

2. If we eat Jesus' Body and drink his Blood, we will have eternal life.

3. Jesus died for us, and he will come again.

 WHAT DO YOU KNOW?

List three things you learned about the Eucharist today.

1._____

2._____

3._____

List three promises Jesus made about the Eucharist.

1._____

2._____

3._____

In Short

- The Bible describes the first Eucharist in the Last Supper.
- The Real Presence of Jesus is in the Eucharist.
- We listen for the call to imitate Christ.

Journey of Faith for Children, Catechumenate, C5 (826344)
Imprimi Potest: Stephen T. Rehrauer, CSsR, Provincial, Denver Province, the Redemptorists.
Imprimatur: "In accordance with CIC 827, permission to publish has been granted on May 3, 2017, by Bishop Mark S. Rivituso, Vicar General, Archdiocese of St. Louis. Permission to publish is an indication that nothing contrary to Church teaching is contained in this work. It does not imply any endorsement of the opinions expressed in the publication, nor is any liability assumed by this permission."
Journey of Faith © 2000, 2017 Liguori Publications. Liguori, MO 63057. To order, visit Liguori.org or call 800-325-9521. Liguori Publications, a nonprofit corporation, is an apostolate of the Redemptorists. To learn more about the Redemptorists, visit Redemptorists.com. All rights reserved. No part of this publication may be reproduced, distributed, stored, transmitted, or posted in any form by any means without prior written permission.
Editors of the 2017 *Journey of Faith for Children:* Theresa Nienaber-Panuski and Pat Fosarelli, MD, DMin.
Design and production: Wendy Barnes, Lorena Mitre Jimenez, John Krus, and Bill Townsend. Illustration: Jeff Albrecht.
Unless noted, Scripture texts in this work are taken from the *New American Bible,* revised edition © 2000, 1991, 1986, 1970 Confraternity of Christian Doctrine, Washington, D.C., and are used by permission of the copyright owner. All Rights Reserved. No part of the *New American Bible* may be reproduced in any form without permission in writing from the copyright owner. Excerpts from the English translation of the *Catechism of the Catholic Church for the United States of America* © 1994 United States Catholic Conference, Inc.—*Libreria Editrice Vaticana;* English translation of the *Catechism of the Catholic Church: Modifications from the Editio Typica* © 1997 United States Catholic Conference, Inc.—*Libreria Editrice Vaticana.* Compliant with *The Roman Missal, Third Edition.*
Printed in the United States of America. 21 20 19 18 17 / 5 4 3 2 1. Third Edition.

Liguori PUBLICATIONS
A Redemptorist Ministry

Closing Prayer

Close this lesson with the prayer below. Ask the children to repeat each line after you.

Lord, help us
to take you at your word,
to trust when we feel confused
and to accept in the faith
that we, too, may come to know
the treasure you have given us
in your own Body and Blood,
broken and poured out for our sins.
You have become for us the food
of everlasting life.
Amen.

Take-Home

Encourage the children and their parents (or godparents or sponsors) to attend eucharistic adoration together the next time your parish offers it.

C6: The Sacrament of Penance and Reconciliation

Catechism: 1420–98

Objectives

- Recognize that no sin is hidden from God.
- Discover sin has consequences beyond the individual.
- Discover the scriptural context for penance.

Leader Meditation

Luke 15:11–32

As you read the parable of the Prodigal Son, first put yourself in the place of the father. Respond with the father's reaction. Do the same with the older son and the younger son. Consider how many times you have been placed in similar positions. When have you yearned for forgiveness? When have you been hurt by someone you love deeply?

Leader Preparation

- Read the lesson, this lesson plan, the Scripture passage, and the *Catechism* sections.
- If possible, arrange to have participants see the reconciliation room or confessional area following the lesson.
- Make copies of a version of the Act of Contrition for the children to use as part of the closing prayer (a version has been included in this lesson's Closing Prayer section). If you're able to do so, print the prayer on card stock or have it laminated and encourage the children to bring it with them when they celebrate the sacrament of penance.
- Be familiar with the following vocabulary terms: confessional, penance, absolve. The definitions are in this guide's glossary.

Welcome

Greet the children as they arrive. Check for supplies and immediate needs. Solicit questions or comments about the previous session and/or share new information and findings. Begin promptly.

Opening Scripture

Luke 15:11–32

Light the candle and read aloud. Before you begin your lesson, ask the children what they think it means to "forgive" and "be forgiven."

> Those who approach the sacrament of Penance obtain pardon from God's mercy for the offense committed against [God], and are, at the same time, reconciled with the Church.
> CCC 1422

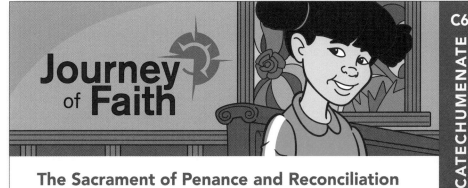

The Sacrament of Penance and Reconciliation

Terrence and Tomás were best friends. They played basketball and rode bikes together. They even built a secret fort in Tomás' back yard. But one day they got in a fight. Terrence was angry so he threw Tomás' ball into the neighbor's yard. The neighbor's dog chewed it up.

Tomás was really angry. Tomás told Terrence he never wanted to play with him again.

Now Terrence and Tomás don't even talk to each other. Terrence misses his friend and feels sad and lonely. Tomás is sad, too. Terrence's mom told him he should say he's sorry, but now Terrence is worried Tomás will never forgive him.

CCC 1420–98

The Sacrament of Penance and Reconciliation

Answer the reflection questions as a group. If you want a more lively activity, you can have small groups act out how they would have Terrence and Tomás solve their problem.

The Brother Who Ran Away

Depending on the ages of the children in your group, you may want to read the parable directly from the Bible (Luke 15:11–24).

As a group, answer the reflection question by making a list of ways you can say, "I'm sorry." Remind students of the ways they can say, "I love you" list they made previously. They can say, "I'm sorry" in ways other than just using those exact words.

Some possible responses include: writing someone an apology note or trying to make the situation right (like giving back something you stole, admitting you lied, or taking the blame for something you did but blamed on someone else).

If you were Terrence, what would you do?

If you were Tomás, what would you do?

Friendship With God and Others

It's sad when our actions hurt our friends. Friendship is important. When we are lonely or sad, happy or excited, it's good to have a friend to turn to. That's why Jesus tells us to love one another. He knows that the secret to happiness is keeping our friendships strong. We do this by saying we're sorry and forgiving when bad things happen.

God is the best friend we have. God will never abandon us. The secret of God's friendship is forgiveness.

Here is a story Jesus told about how God forgives.

The Brother Who Ran Away

Once there was a brother who wanted to live on his own. He asked his father for his share of the family's money and left his home.

He traveled all over. He only did things he wanted to do. He made a lot of friends who showed him new ways to spend his money. But the money didn't last forever. One day the brother found he spent all his money. There was nothing left. He turned to his friends for help, but they had all left him.

He thought about his father and older brother. It was time to go home. "I'll tell my father I'm really sorry and ask if I can sleep in his barn. I'll tend his sheep and do all that he asks me, if only he will take me back again," he thought.

When the father saw his son in the distance, he ran to greet him with open arms. "Call my friends," he said. "We'll have a party for my son was lost and now has come home."

Adapted from Luke 15:11–24

Jesus told this story to teach us that no matter how far from God we wander, our loving Father waits for us to come back.

What are some ways you can tell someone you're sorry?

Already Forgiven

Did you notice that even before the son said, "I'm sorry," the father had forgiven him? That's like us and God. In the sacrament of penance, we can talk about things we are sorry for and for things we wish we never did. The priest reminds us of God's loving mercy and tells us a way to fix our friendship with God and anyone we might have hurt.

Read these stories about Jesus' forgiveness.

- Luke 7:36–50

How did the woman say she was sorry?

What did Jesus do?

- Luke 19:1–10

How did Zacchaeus say he was sorry?

What did Jesus do?

What Happens in Reconciliation?

1. Enter the **confessional**, a small room or space where the priest is seated.

2. Greet the priest and say, "Bless me Father, for I have sinned." Then tell the priest that it's your first confession (or how long it has been since your last confession).

3. Name any sins you are sorry for. Don't worry about listing each one in detail. Just explain what you did and why you feel sorry for it.

4. Listen carefully to the advice the priest gives you.

5. The priest will give you a penance. A **penance** is a simple action or prayer you can do to help make up for what you did and heal your friendships. Your penance will also help you grow closer to God.

6. Say an Act of Contrition prayer. Your catechist or the priest will give you a copy.

7. The priest will pray over you and God, through the priest, will **absolve**, or erase, your sins through a special prayer of absolution that ends with a Sign of the Cross. This sign also gives you special grace to live more like Jesus.

8. You really are forgiven! Thank the priest as you leave, and go do your penance!

What Happens in Reconciliation?

As you begin this section, mention to candidates that they can receive the sacrament of reconciliation now and that this may be something they want to do before receiving the Eucharist and entering full communion with the Church. (If you've already planned a group penance day prior to the Easter Vigil, let the children know when that is. If not, let children and their sponsors know when your parish celebrates the sacrament of penance.)

Remind the catechumens that, while they won't be able to receive the sacrament of reconciliation yet, their sins will be forgiven at their baptism. You can still invite them to any group reconciliation time you have planned, and instead of participating in the sacrament you can ask the catechumens to pray an examination of conscience quietly to help prepare them for their baptism.

If you scheduled time for the children to see your parish's confessionals or reconciliation rooms, this is a good time to transition out of your regular space. If your scheduled time is at the beginning of class, consider starting your lesson with this section so the children can visualize.

If it's possible to have your pastor or another parish priest teach this part of the lesson, ask him to walk the children through the sacrament and encourage them to visit him again on their own for the sacrament. (Even some adults can be nervous about going to penance, so try to make the sacrament seem as approachable as possible.)

Already Forgiven

Divide the children into two groups and assign each group one of the Scripture passages in this section to work on. In a small group, you can have children work individually and then share their answers. If you have a large group, you can have multiple groups of three or four children for each Scripture passage.

• Luke 7:36–50

How did the woman say she was sorry? *She washed Jesus' feet with her tears and dried them with her hair (a sign of her humility and repentance) and then she anointed his feet with ointment.*

What did Jesus do? *Jesus forgave her because of her faith. The woman showed Jesus she was truly sorry for the wrong things she'd done, and she showed Jesus that she truly believed in him and his power to forgive her sins.*

• Luke 19:1–10

How did Zacchaeus say he was sorry? *He told Jesus he would give half of whatever he had to the poor and repay any money he had illegally taken (extorted) from others.*

What did Jesus do? *Jesus saw that Zacchaeus was truly sorry for the wrong things he'd done, and he forgave Zacchaeus.*

Final Activity

Let the children complete the activity on their own. After all the children have decoded the message, ask them which story they read today used this phrase and what it meant.

The answer to the decoded message: He was lost and has been found.

This message is from the parable of the Prodigal Son in Luke 19:24. The father is saying that, while his son was lost to him and out committing sins with no regret, his son had now returned to him asking forgiveness and feeling truly sorry for what he'd done. The father rejoices when his son returns, just like our heavenly Father rejoices when we ask for forgiveness in the sacrament of penance.

DECODE THE MESSAGE

Cross out every other letter below. Use the remaining letters to complete the sentence.

HVER   WLAOS   KLCOYSKTB   AMNPDI   HUAZS

BBIEFEMN   EFUOOUVNSD

" _____ _____   _____ _____ _____   _____ _____ _____

_____ _____ _____   _____ _____ _____   _____ _____ _____ _____

_____ _____   _____ _____ _____."

(Luke 15:24, 32)

In Short

- Sin isn't hidden from God.
- Sin has consequences beyond yourself.
- Scripture supports penance.

Journey of Faith for Children, Catechumenate, C6 (826344)
Imprimi Potest: Stephen T. Rehrauer, CSsR, Provincial, Denver Province, the Redemptorists.
Imprimatur: "In accordance with CIC 827, permission to publish has been granted on May 3, 2017, by Bishop Mark S. Rivituso, Vicar General, Archdiocese of St. Louis. Permission to publish is an indication that nothing contrary to Church teaching is contained in this work. It does not imply any endorsement of the opinions expressed in the publication, nor is any liability assumed by this permission."
Journey of Faith © 2000, 2017 Liguori Publications, Liguori, MO 63057. To order, visit Liguori.org or call 800-325-9521. Liguori Publications, a nonprofit corporation, is an apostolate of the Redemptorists. To learn more about the Redemptorists, visit Redemptorists.com. All rights reserved. No part of this publication may be reproduced, distributed, stored, transmitted, or posted in any form by any means without prior written permission.
Editors of the 2017 *Journey of Faith for Children:* Theresa Nienaber-Panuski and Pat Fosarelli, MD, DMin.
Design and production: Wendy Barnes, Lorena Mitre Jimenez, John Krus, and Bill Townsend. Illustration: Jeff Albrecht.
Unless noted, Scripture texts in this work are taken from the *New American Bible*, revised edition © 2000, 1991, 1986, 1970 Confraternity of Christian Doctrine, Washington, D.C., and are used by permission of the copyright owner. All Rights Reserved. No part of the *New American Bible* may be reproduced in any form without permission in writing from the copyright owner. Excerpts from the English translation of the *Catechism of the Catholic Church* for the United States of America © 1994 United States Catholic Conference, Inc.—Libreria Editrice Vaticana; English translation of the *Catechism of the Catholic Church:* Modifications from the *Editio Typica* © 1997 United States Catholic Conference, Inc.—Libreria Editrice Vaticana. Compliant with *The Roman Missal, Third Edition.*
Printed in the United States of America. 21 20 19 18 17 / 5 4 3 2 1. Third Edition.

Liguori
PUBLICATIONS
A Redemptorist Ministry

Closing Prayer

Hand out the Act of Contrition prayer (at right) to the children. We have modernized a few words to make the prayer easier for the children to pray on their own. If you use a different version than the one here, pray the version you've provided to the group instead.

Take-Home

Ask the children to practice the Act of Contrition by saying it each night before they go to bed this week. Encourage the children to say the prayer while reflecting on their actions of that day.

Act of Contrition Prayer

O my God, I am very sorry for having offended you, and I hate all my sins, because of your just punishments, but most of all because they offend you, my God, who is all good and deserving of my love. I firmly resolve with the help of your grace to sin no more and to avoid the near occasion of sin. Amen.

C7: The Sacrament of Anointing of the Sick

Catechism: 1499–1532

Objectives

- Discover that the sacrament of anointing has its roots in Jesus' ministry on earth, and examples of this ministry can be found in the New Testament.
- Outline the basic steps in the sacrament.
- Describe the nature of the sacrament as going beyond "last rites" or preparation for death.

Leader Meditation

James 5:13–16

The early Church saw a great connection between the healing of the body and the healing of the soul. In this lesson, children will be asked to make a distinction between curing and healing. Reflect on this sacrament's emphasis on restored spiritual and emotional health.

Leader Preparation

- Read the lesson, this lesson plan, the Scripture passage, and the *Catechism* sections.
- If you can, display the blessed oil used in anointing of the sick.
- Be familiar with the following vocabulary terms: anointing of the sick, holy oil, curing, healing. The definitions are in this guide's glossary.

Welcome

Greet the children as they arrive. Check for supplies and immediate needs. Solicit questions or comments about the previous session and/or share new information and findings. Begin promptly.

Opening Scripture

James 5:13–16

Light the candle and read aloud. If you were able to bring sacred oil for today's lesson, pass it around the room and explain that this oil was blessed by a bishop and is an important symbol connected with this lesson's sacrament.

> By the sacred anointing of the sick and the prayer of the priests the whole Church commends those who are ill to the suffering and glorified Lord, that he may raise them up and save them.
>
> CCC 1499

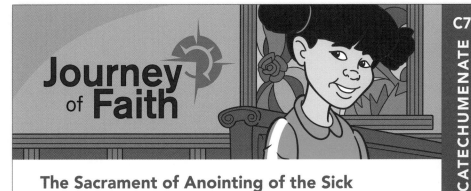

The Sacrament of Anointing of the Sick

"Any special intentions?" Mrs. Evans asked.

Lisa raised her hand. "For my grandma. She's been really sick. A priest came over yesterday to say some prayers and put oil on her hands."

"That's called the anointing of the sick," Mrs. Evans said. "That means the Holy Spirit, through the priest, gave your grandma special grace to help with her sickness."

CCC 1499–1532

The Sacrament of Anointing of the Sick

After reading the story, ask the children to write down the name of someone they know who is sick or needs prayers. You will pray for these people during this lesson's closing prayer. If you prefer, you can ask the children to write down the name of the person they'd like to pray for on a folded-up piece of paper and hand it in. Then you can read these names during the closing prayer.

Jesus Heals With Love

Depending on the average age of the children in your group, you may want to read the Scripture account in Mark 2:1–12.

Four Steps to Healing

Go over these four steps with your group. Ask the children if they can remember another sacrament you talked about that uses the laying on of hands and anointing with holy oil. *Confirmation.*

Ask the children if they remember what those signs meant in the sacrament of confirmation. *That we receive the Holy Spirit in a special way and are given the command to go out and bring God's good news to the world.*

Then ask the children what they think these symbols might mean for this sacrament. *That we are receiving special grace from the Holy Spirit, that we are receiving Jesus in a special way.*

Do you know anyone who is sick and needs special prayers?

Jesus Heals With Love

One day, Jesus was teaching at a house in Capernaum. So many people came to hear him that they filled the house. Then four men came up to the house. They were carrying their friend on a stretcher. He was paralyzed. The men wanted Jesus to heal their friend, but they couldn't get inside. So they climbed up to the roof, opened up part of it, and lowered their friend down to Jesus. Jesus looked at their friend and said, "Your sins are forgiven." Then Jesus told the man to stand up and go home. The man picked up his stretcher and walked out. All the people were amazed and praised Jesus.

Adapted from Mark 2:1–12

Four Steps to Healing

The sacrament of **anointing of the sick** is God's way of healing people with the same loving touch that Jesus used when he healed people on earth.

STEP 1

Someone reads from the Bible about how Jesus healed the sick and helped those who sinned. As we listen, we remember that Jesus can heal our bodies and souls.

STEP 2

The priest places his hands on the head of the person receiving the sacrament. He invites the Holy Spirit to come into the person's heart. We remember that Jesus always prayed and touched the people he healed.

STEP 3

The priest says a prayer of blessing over the holy oil. The **holy oil** prepares the sick person for the Holy Spirit. We are also anointed with oil at our baptism and confirmation.

STEP 4

The priest makes the Sign of the Cross on the forehead of the person being anointed. We remember that Jesus suffered on the cross. The priest also anoints the person's hands. We remember that our hands do Jesus' work on earth.

Tomas' Grandpa: A Story About Anointing

"Can I talk about what happened to my grandpa?" Tomás asked.

Mrs. Evans nodded.

"Well, my grandpa was really sick and he wanted a priest to come over and pray with him," Tomás said. "The priest did all the anointing of the sick stuff. I thought it was going to make him better.

"Our whole family was there. We stood around Grandpa's bed and prayed while the priest anointed his hands and feet. My grandpa reminded us that God loves all of us and he loved God. Then my grandpa said he was at peace and was glad his whole family was with him.

"But then he died," Tomás said, frowning. "I thought the priest was supposed to make him better. I was really mad at the priest and at God. Why didn't he get better if he had the sacrament?"

"That's a really tough question, Tomás," Mrs. Evans said. "It hurts when the people we care about die. We miss them a lot. We wonder why God didn't just make them better. But God loves all of us very much. When anointing of the sick doesn't make someone better, that doesn't mean the sacrament didn't work. It means God is helping that person in a different way and that God will be helping that person on the journey to be with him in heaven."

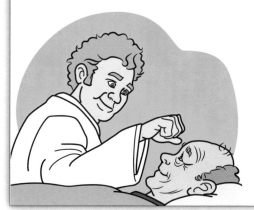

Will Anointing Heal the Person?

Healing someone isn't the same as curing someone. **Curing** takes away the disease or physical disability. **Healing** goes deeper. When someone is healed through the anointing of the sick, he or she receives:

- the courage and strength to suffer, just as Jesus had the courage and strength to endure his crucifixion.

- grace that prepares her soul, mind, and body to meet Jesus in heaven.

- the special peace that comes from knowing he is forgiven and that everything is going to be all right.

- a reminder that God is always watching over us.

Sometimes, someone may be cured through the sacrament of anointing of the sick. But even if someone does not receive a cure, God still cares about that person and is preparing her or him for something greater.

Write down the name of someone you know who is sick.

_____

Say a special prayer for this person now. Remember the person in your prayers this week.

It was an important time for all of Tomás' family to be together, and knowing his grandpa received the sacrament may have made other people in Tomás' family feel at peace, too.

We celebrate a lot of sacraments with our loved ones! At our baptism, we celebrate especially with our godparents who promise to be our guides in faith. At the Eucharist, we share a meal with all the members of our Church family. At confirmation, we celebrate with the whole Church and especially our sponsor. At marriage and holy orders (which will be discussed in more detail in upcoming lessons), we commit to serving a specific vocation in a special way in front of our loved ones.

Will Anointing Heal the Person?

After reading this section, ask children if they want to change their definitions of "healing" and "curing."

Emphasize that anyone who is very sick can receive the sacrament of anointing. It is not just a sacrament for people who are dying. In fact, a lot of people who receive this sacrament do go on to recover.

Give the children time to respond to the reflection question on their own. Remind them of the name they wrote at the beginning of the lesson. They can use this name or write down a second.

Tomás' Grandpa: A Story About Anointing

The children may find it difficult to talk about illness and death if it's something that reminds them of a difficult experience or if it's something they haven't experienced firsthand. As you read this story, you can ask the children questions about Tomás' experience, which will give them a frame of reference without the conversation getting too personal.

After you've read the story, ask the children what they think the difference between "healing" and "curing" might be.

Curing is making someone's body better. Healing is making someone's soul better or at peace. Jesus both cured and healed people in the Bible, but sometimes God doesn't cure people. That doesn't mean God loves those people less than others.

Then ask the children why they think it was important for all of Tomás' family to be there for the sacrament and not just Tomás' grandpa alone. If the children need prompting to help answer this question, ask them what other sacraments are celebrated with our families or other people we care about.

Final Activity

Give the children time to complete this activity on their own or with a partner. Walk around as the children work to affirm correct answers and clarify any points of confusion. The answers are in red type below.

1. Jesus forgives the paralyzed man's sins and helps him walk again.

     Healing and Curing

2. Jesus gives the blind man his sight back.

     Curing

3. A doctor sets someone's broken leg and the leg gets better.

     Curing

4. A person with cancer is very depressed. A priest prays with the person and he begins to feel better but is still sick.

     Healing

5. You're sad because your grandpa is sick. You pray with your grandpa and start to feel better.

     Healing

6. Your friend has a fever, but after taking some medicine your friend is ready to go back to school.

     Curing

HEALING OR CURING?

Think about each scenario and decide if it's healing, curing, or both. Then write the number of the action in the matching circle.

1. Jesus forgives the paralyzed man's sins and helps him walk again.
2. Jesus gives the blind man his sight back.
3. A doctor sets someone's broken leg and the leg gets better.
4. A person with cancer is very depressed. A priest prays with them and they begin to feel better, but the person is still sick.
5. You're sad because your grandpa is sick. You pray with your grandpa and start to feel better.
6. Your friend has a fever, but after taking some medicine your friend is ready to go back to school.

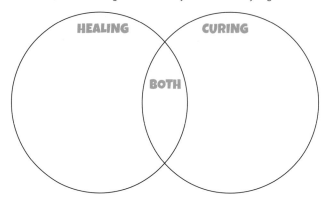

In Short

- Anointing stems from Jesus' healing ministry.
- The sacrament follows basic steps.
- The sacrament is more than preparation for death.

Journey of Faith for Children, Catechumenate, C7 (826344)
Imprimi Potest: Stephen T. Rehrauer, CSsR, Provincial, Denver Province, the Redemptorists.
Imprimatur: "In accordance with CIC 827, permission to publish has been granted on May 3, 2017, by Bishop Mark S. Rivituso, Vicar General, Archdiocese of St. Louis. Permission to publish is an indication that nothing contrary to Church teaching is contained in this work. It does not imply any endorsement of the opinions expressed in the publication, nor is any liability assumed by this permission."
Journey of Faith © 2000, 2017 Liguori Publications, Liguori, MO 63057. To order, visit Liguori.org or call 800-325-9521. Liguori Publications, a nonprofit corporation, is an apostolate of the Redemptorists. To learn more about the Redemptorists, visit Redemptorists.com. All rights reserved. No part of this publication may be reproduced, distributed, stored, transmitted, or posted in any form by any means without prior written permission.
Editors of the 2017 *Journey of Faith for Children:* Theresa Nienaber-Panuski and Pat Fosarelli, MD, DMin.
Design and production: Wendy Barnes, Lorena Mitre Jimenez, John Krus, and Bill Townsend. Illustration: Jeff Albrecht.
Unless noted, Scripture texts in this work are taken from the *New American Bible,* revised edition © 2000, 1991, 1986, 1970 Confraternity of Christian Doctrine, Washington, D.C., and are used by permission of the copyright owner. All Rights Reserved. No part of the *New American Bible* may be reproduced in any form without permission in writing from the copyright owner. Excerpts from the English translation of the *Catechism of the Catholic Church* for the United States of America © 1994 United States Catholic Conference, Inc.—*Libreria Editrice Vaticana;* English translation of the *Catechism of the Catholic Church: Modifications from the Editio Typica* © 1997 United States Catholic Conference, Inc.—*Libreria Editrice Vaticana.*
Compliant with *The Roman Missal, Third Edition.*
Printed in the United States of America. 21 20 19 18 17 / 5 4 3 2 1. Third Edition.

Liguori
PUBLICATIONS
A Redemptorist Ministry

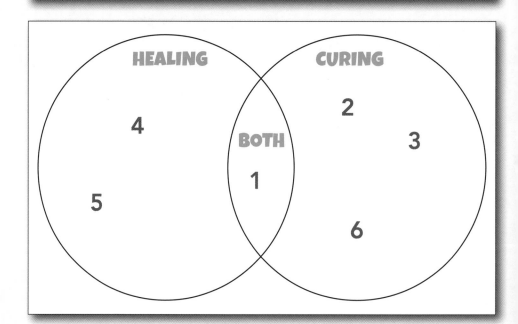

Closing Prayer

Ask each child to read (or you read aloud) the name of the person he or she would like to pray for today. Of if you prefer, you can read the list of names that will be read during Universal Prayer at Mass the following Sunday. Pray the Our Father as a group.

Take-Home

Ask the children to take their special intention home to their family and lead their family in prayer for this person each night (or morning) this week.

C8: The Sacrament of Matrimony

Catechism: 1533–35, 1601–66

Objectives

- Identify ways sacramental marriage reflects the paschal mystery.
- Identify ways sacramental marriage reflects the love of the Trinity.
- Begin to list the spiritual characteristics of marriage.

Leader Meditation

Colossians 3:12–17

How does this passage encourage us to treat one another? Consider not only spouses but friends, coworkers, neighbors, and more. Consider your own attitudes toward marriage and the blessings, as well as the difficulties, you may have encountered in relationships.

Leader Preparation

- Read the lesson, this lesson plan, the Scripture passage, and the *Catechism* sections. As you read this lesson, be particularly sensitive to the feelings of the children who may have parents who are recently divorced, separated, or remarried, as well as the feelings of the children who may be from nontraditional households.

- Be familiar with the following vocabulary terms: sacrament of matrimony, vows, wedding rings, annulment. The definitions are in this guide's glossary.

Welcome

Greet the children as they arrive. Check for supplies and immediate needs. Solicit questions or comments about the previous session and/or share new information and findings. Begin promptly.

Opening Scripture

Colossians 3:12–17

Light the candle and read aloud. Before beginning the lesson handout, ask the children what this passage teaches them about love.

When we love someone we treat that person with kindness and compassion; we are patient and forgiving toward those we love; when we love we are letting Christ dwell within.

> The matrimonial covenant, by which a man and a woman establish between themselves a partnership of the whole of life, ...has been raised by Christ the Lord to the dignity of a sacrament.
>
> *CCC 1601*

The Sacrament of Matrimony

"Today we're going to talk about sacramental marriage," Mrs. Evans said. "So I've brought Mr. Evans with me to help!"

The class was excited to have a visitor for the day and to hear about Mrs. and Mr. Evans' life outside of class.

"Why did you decide to get married?" Lisa asked.

"Is there a difference between Catholic marriage and other kinds of marriages?" Terrence asked.

"Did you have a big party with your families?" Tomás wanted to know.

CCC 1533–35, 1601–66

The Sacrament of Matrimony

Marriage can be a complicated topic to talk about, and depending on what faith tradition or environment the children are coming from, they may have heard a lot of different teachings on marriage and what it stands for.

So as you begin this lesson, ask the children to respond to the reflection question either out loud or by writing their questions on a sheet of paper and handing it in. You may not be able to adequately answer all their questions during this session. For those questions you can't answer, try to follow up after doing some research.

Two Become One, and More

You may want to start the session by having children create a group definition of marriage based on what they know at the beginning of the lesson. They can revise that definition at the end of the session.

Emphasize to the children that a sacramental marriage is about much more than just two people who love each other.

What Happens at a Wedding?

Ask the children if any of them have ever been to a wedding and what they remember about that wedding. As you read through the section, you can call attention to any elements that are similar to the weddings the children described to make the sacrament seem more familiar.

Give the children time to complete the reflection question with a partner, small group, or all together.

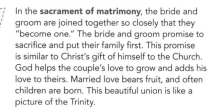

What questions do you have about marriage as a sacrament?

Two Become One, and More

Marriage begins with two people in love. One man and one woman. These two people want to share their whole lives with each other.

Jesus grew up with Mary and Joseph. Jesus saw every day how their love for each other made their family strong, happy, and faith-filled.

Later, Jesus taught a deeper truth of marriage:

"From the beginning of creation, 'God made them male and female. For this reason a man shall leave his father and mother and be joined to his wife, and the two shall become one flesh.' So they are no longer two but one flesh."

Mark 10:6–8

In the **sacrament of matrimony**, the bride and groom are joined together so closely that they "become one." The bride and groom promise to sacrifice and put their family first. This promise is similar to Christ's gift of himself to the Church. God helps the couple's love to grow and adds his love to theirs. Married love bears fruit, and often children are born. This beautiful union is like a picture of the Trinity.

What Happens at a Wedding?

Many weddings happen during a Mass. Even those that don't happen during a Mass usually begin with readings from the Bible. Then the bride and groom stand before the altar and speak their vows. **Vows** are their promises to each other. The bride and groom promise to love one another forever, "in good times and in bad, in sickness and in health," even "for richer, for poorer" (*The Rite of Marriage*). Then they exchange rings. In the sacrament of matrimony, **wedding rings** are a sign of a couple's everlasting bond.

Marriage is different from all the other sacraments. The bride and groom perform the sacrament themselves! Once they both state their vows, they are officially married. The priest or deacon stands as the Church's witness and leads other parts of the ceremony.

What do you think it takes to be married for life? List some of those things below.

_____

_____

_____

_____

_____

_____

_____

Married for Life

When two people get married before God, their marriage is for life. It takes a lot of hard work to live out that love every day. They need God's help, too.

But sometimes a marriage ends in divorce. After a divorce, the Church looks at the marriage to see if a husband and wife really meant the promises they made at their wedding. If they were too young, didn't understand what their vows meant, or didn't mean to keep their vows, the Church will give them an annulment. An **annulment** says the marriage wasn't actually a sacrament because something essential to that marriage was missing.

After an annulment is granted, both people are free to get married. If a person does remarry, the Church will bless the new union as a sacrament.

Even if a marriage ends in a divorce or divorce and annulment, God is still present with that family. God doesn't stop loving parents or children just because a marriage wasn't a sacrament. Any arrangements separated parents make about where they will live or who their children will live with should be made with the same love God has for them.

Other Types of Unions

Sometimes two men, two women, or even more than two people will ask to be married or joined in a union together. A union like this may be legal, but it can never be a sacramental marriage because that can only occur between one man and one woman.

Married love both keeps a family together and makes it grow through the birth and raising of children. Christian husbands and wives promise to accept children into their family. This union of two people creating new life is God's image of marriage.

Married Forever

As you discuss this section, be particularly sensitive to the children who may have parents who are divorced and possibly remarried. Emphasize that the children are never to blame for the end of a marriage and that it is not the child's responsibility to determine whether or not their parents' marriage should have been annulled.

Also emphasize that even if a marriage is annulled, children from that marriage are still their parents' children. Nothing changes that.

Other Types of Unions

As you read through this section, go back to the beginning of this lesson and reread the Scripture passage from Mark 10:6–8 that states we are made male and female to be husband and wife, mother and father.

Stress the difference between a legal union (one recognized by the state) and a sacramental union (a union recognized by the Church). There is an opportunity to broaden the discussion here by saying there are some things that are legal that go against the laws we're given by God. As Catholics, it is important for us to follow God's laws first.

As you end the session, go back to your group definition of marriage and ask the children how they'd change it (or if they'd leave it the same) after today's lesson.

Final Activity

This activity may be difficult for the children to complete during the session, so encourage them to complete it on their own time. They can ask their parents' these questions, or their godparents or sponsor (if married), or another relative or family friend.

THE NEWS AROUND TOWN

Pretend you are a reporter. Find a married couple and ask them about their marriage. Write down what you find out.

Here are some questions to start with:

- How did you meet?
- How long did you date before you decided to get married?
- What's the best thing about being married?
- What's the hardest thing about being married?
- How is God a part of your marriage?

In Short

- Marriage reflects the paschal mystery.
- Marriage reflects the love of the Trinity.
- Marriage has many spiritual characteristics.

Journey of Faith for Children, Catechumenate, C8 (826344)

Imprimi Potest: Stephen T. Rehrauer, CSsR, Provincial, Denver Province, the Redemptorists.

Imprimatur: "In accordance with CIC 827, permission to publish has been granted on May 3, 2017, by Bishop Mark S. Rivituso, Vicar General, Archdiocese of St. Louis. Permission to publish is an indication that nothing contrary to Church teaching is contained in this work. It does not imply any endorsement of the opinions expressed in the publication, nor is any liability assumed by this permission."

Journey of Faith © 2000, 2017 Liguori Publications, Liguori, MO 63057. To order, visit Liguori.org or call 800-325-9521. Liguori Publications, a nonprofit corporation, is an apostolate of the Redemptorists. To learn more about the Redemptorists, visit Redemptorists.com. All rights reserved. No part of this publication may be reproduced, distributed, stored, transmitted, or posted in any form by any means without prior written permission.

Editors of the 2017 *Journey of Faith for Children:* Theresa Nienaber-Panuski and Pat Fosarelli, MD, DMin.

Design and production: Wendy Barnes, Lorena Mitre Jimenez, John Krus, and Bill Townsend. Illustration: Jeff Albrecht.

Unless noted, Scripture texts in this work are taken from the *New American Bible,* revised edition © 2000, 1991, 1986, 1970 Confraternity of Christian Doctrine, Washington, D.C., and are used by permission of the copyright owner. All Rights Reserved. No part of the *New American Bible* may be reproduced in any form without permission in writing from the copyright owner. Excerpts from the English translation of the *Catechism of the Catholic Church for the United States of America* © 1994 United States Catholic Conference, Inc.—Libreria Editrice Vaticana; English translation of the *Catechism of the Catholic Church: Modifications from the Editio Typica* © 1997 United States Catholic Conference, Inc.—Libreria Editrice Vaticana. Compliant with *The Roman Missal, Third Edition.*

Printed in the United States of America. 21 20 19 18 17 / 5 4 3 2 1. Third Edition.

Liguori PUBLICATIONS
A Redemptorist Ministry

Closing Prayer

Ask the children to silently call to mind their parents and any other relationships that have helped them better understand the love of God. Then read 1 Corinthians 13:1–7 as a closing meditation.

Take-Home

For this session's take-home, ask the children to complete the final activity in "The News Around Town."

C9: The Sacrament of Holy Orders

Catechism: 1536–1600

Objectives

- List the three separate degrees of holy orders.
- Recognize holy orders is rooted in the Scriptures and the traditions of the early Church.
- Define the diaconate as the first step of the ordained priesthood.

Leader Meditation

Mark 10:43–45

Reflect on Jesus' message that to serve others is to serve God. As an RCIA leader, you are serving God by teaching the young men and women under your guidance. Ask our Lord for the wisdom and grace to serve them well.

Leader Preparation

- Read the lesson, this lesson plan, the Scripture passage, and the *Catechism* sections.
- Find a musical rendition of "Here I Am, Lord" for the closing prayer (if you can't find a recording or can't play music in your room, you can read the verse from Scripture, 1 Samuel 3:7–10, instead).
- See if your pastor, another parish priest, or a deacon is available to be a guest for this session.
- Be familiar with the following vocabulary terms: holy orders, ordained, clergy, transitional deacons, permanent deacons. The definitions are in this guide's glossary.

Welcome

Greet the children as they arrive. Check for supplies and immediate needs. Solicit questions or comments about the previous session and/or share new information and findings. Begin promptly.

Opening Scripture

Mark 10:43–45

Light the candle and read aloud. Emphasize that service to others is one of Jesus' commands. We serve God best by serving God's people.

> The sacrament of Holy Orders communicates a "sacred power" which is none other than that of Christ. The exercise of this authority must therefore be measured against the model of Christ, who by love made himself the least and servant of all.
>
> CCC 1551

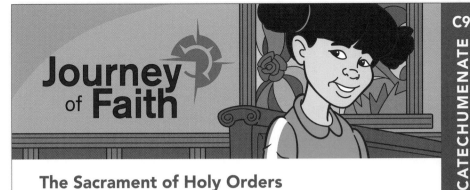

The Sacrament of Holy Orders

"Do priests ever get lonely?" Terrence asked. "I only ever see our priest at church, and he lives all by himself. I think I'd be pretty lonely."

"I met a deacon who was married! He even had kids! Why don't priests get to have families?" Lisa asked.

"Priests do have families, most especially they are part of Christ's family, the Church, and they lead all of us in our faith," Mrs. Evans answered.

CCC 1536–1600

C9

The Sacrament of Holy Orders

After reading the story, ask the children to write down their questions about priests or deacons and give them to you or, if you have a guest speaker today, let him talk about his experience being ordained and invite the children to ask their questions directly to him.

Encourage the children to be serious but honest with their questions. Even questions like, "Why do priests dress like that?" can lead to rich discussions about Church traditions and the faith when asked sincerely.

The Work of the Apostles

If questions about why only men can be priests in the Catholic Church come up, point children to the example of the twelve apostles, the men who learned from Jesus directly and did his work on earth. While Jesus had many female followers, he gave his apostles specific instructions on how to lead and build his church. This does not mean women are less important than men in the Catholic Church. Just look at the example of Mary, Jesus' own Mother!

As you go through the three points in this section, ask the children if they can think of any sacraments you've previously discussed that seem to fall under those categories.

1. The holy Eucharist, which is celebrated in the context of the Mass.

2. Penance and reconciliation, where Jesus forgives our sins through the priest.

3. Baptism, bringing sheep into the fold of the Church, and anointing of the sick, where Jesus through the priest gives special grace to those suffering from physical illnesses.

Emphasize to the children that priests don't do anything of their own power. It is Jesus working through them that allows priests to perform the sacraments. Priests become Jesus' hands and voice in the Church by teaching us about God, healing us when we're sick, giving us absolution when we repent, and feeding us with the Eucharist.

? *What questions do you have about being a priest or deacon?*

The Work of the Apostles

Jesus called twelve apostles to share his work on earth. He taught them a lot! Then he gave them power and sent them out to share the good news, help the poor, heal the sick, and forgive sins.

Men who choose to serve God and his Church with their lives receive the sacrament of **holy orders**. During holy orders, these men are **ordained**. That means they have been chosen, and the Holy Spirit will prepare them for their work. Priests carry Jesus to the world in three special ways:

1. They Celebrate the Mass

"Jesus took bread, said the blessing, broke it, and [gave] it to his disciples.... Then he took a cup, gave thanks, and gave it to them...."

Matthew 26:26–28

At the Last Supper, Jesus told his apostles to "do this in memory of me" (Luke 22:19). Every day, priests around the world speak and act in memory of Jesus. They act through the power and person of Christ. Just as Jesus commanded them to. When the priest says, "This is my body" and "This is my blood," Jesus is speaking to us through him.

2. They Forgive Sins

After Jesus was raised from the dead, he appeared to his apostles and said:

"'As the Father has sent me, so I send you.' And when he had said this, he breathed on them and said to them, 'Receive the holy Spirit. Whose sins you forgive are forgiven them, and whose sins you retain are retained.'"

John 20:21–23

In a similar way, when a priest absolves you by saying the words of forgiveness in the sacrament of penance, that sin isn't just forgotten. It is removed by the power of God's mercy. Just like Jesus speaks through the priest during the Eucharist, God forgives us through the priest during penance and reconciliation.

3. They Care for God's Flock

Jesus said:

"I am the good shepherd. A good shepherd lays down his life for the sheep.... I know mine and mine know me, just as the Father knows me and I know the Father; and I will lay down my life for the sheep."

John 10:11, 14–15

When Jesus said, "Feed my sheep" (John 21:17), he was making Peter the leader of the apostles. Deacons and priests promise to obey their local bishop, and all bishops promise to obey the pope.

Degrees of Holy Orders

All ordained men are called **clergy**. Because ordination has been passed down from Jesus, to Peter, to the apostles, on and on, every member of the clergy is connected to our Christian leaders and ancestors. There are three degrees of ordination.

- *Bishops* are the successors of the apostles. They lead a diocese or special Church office. They explain God's teachings in ways their community can understand. Bishops can celebrate all the sacraments and cannot be married.

- *Priests* are assistants of the local bishop. They lead God's people in worship and give them spiritual guidance. Priests can celebrate the sacraments of baptism, Eucharist, penance, the anointing of the sick, marriage, and sometimes confirmation. Priests cannot be married.

- There are two types of *deacons*. Some deacons are training to be priests. They are called **transitional deacons** because they are transitioning from being a deacon to being a priest. Transitional deacons cannot get married. Some deacons want to remain deacons for life. They are called **permanent deacons**. A permanent deacon might have a wife if he was married before he was ordained. Deacons can be the official Church leader, or witness, at baptisms, marriages, and funerals. Deacons can also preach and assist the priest at Mass.

What Happens During the Sacrament?

During the sacrament of holy orders, some special things happen to the person being ordained:

- *Vesting*, or dressing, in a stole or chasuble. A deacon is vested in a stole and dalmatic. A priest is vested in a chasuble. Wearing this over their clothes is a sign that deacons and priests take on a new identity with their ordination.

- *Laying on of hands.* Jesus laid his hands on his apostles to give them power to carry on his work. The Church has done this ever since! This action shows that Jesus is sharing his power.

- *Anointing of hands.* In the Bible, people were anointed with blessed oil before beginning a special task. The ordained person will also do many special tasks for God.

- *Presentation of chalice or Gospels.* A priest is presented with the chalice he will use at Mass. A deacon is presented with a book of the Gospels he will read at Mass.

Degrees of Holy Orders

This section is another opportunity to give things over to a guest speaker, if you have one, and let him share his firsthand experience of holy orders.

As you discuss these different degrees, ask the children when they think they've seen a deacon, priest, or bishop during Mass. The children may never have seen a bishop during Mass, but they may for their confirmation. Ask the children what they remember the deacon or priest (or bishop) doing during Mass. Connect that to the roles you're discussing here.

What Happens During the Sacrament?

As you go through each action or symbol, ask the children if they can remember that symbol being used in another sacrament you've discussed.

Vesting can be compared to the white garment used at baptism and the exchange of rings in marriage. Both actions are symbols worn to show the individual's (or couple's) commitment to the vocation.

The laying on of hands is used in confirmation and anointing of the sick.

Anointing is used in confirmation (on the head) and anointing of the sick.

Presentation of the *Book of the Gospels* (for deacons) and the presentation of the chalice and paten (for priests) is special to holy orders.

C9

Final Activity

If you have time, complete this final activity as a class. You can encourage the children to think about not just what a priest or deacon needs for himself, but things he might need to perform a sacrament (like a priest would need a chalice and a paten for the Eucharist). The answers will vary based on your group. An example has been given for you in each column.

As an alternate activity, you can ask the children to interview a priest or deacon from your parish (or any they know that would be willing to sit down for an interview) on their own. Some questions have been included below.

What's your favorite thing about being a priest or deacon?

What do you remember most about your ordination?

What kinds of things do you do as a priest or a deacon?

THE RIGHT STUFF!

What do you think it takes to be a priest or deacon? In the first column, list things a priest or deacon might need. In the second column, list qualities of a good priest or deacon. The first row is done for you.

Things a priest or deacon needs	Qualities of a priest or deacon
A copy of the Bible	Good listener

In Short

- Holy orders has three separate degrees.
- Holy orders is rooted in the Bible and the early Church.
- Holy orders is the first step of the ordained priesthood.

Journey of Faith for Children, Catechumenate, C9 (826344)
Imprimi Potest: Stephen T. Rehrauer, CSsR, Provincial, Denver Province, the Redemptorists.
Imprimatur: "In accordance with CIC 827, permission to publish has been granted on May 3, 2017, by Bishop Mark S. Rivituso, Vicar General, Archdiocese of St. Louis. Permission to publish is an indication that nothing contrary to Church teaching is contained in this work. It does not imply any endorsement of the opinions expressed in the publication, nor is any liability assumed by this permission."
Journey of Faith © 2000, 2017 Liguori Publications, Liguori, MO 63057. To order, visit Liguori.org or call 800-325-9521. Liguori Publications, a nonprofit corporation, is an apostolate of the Redemptorists. To learn more about the Redemptorists, visit Redemptorists.com. All rights reserved. No part of this publication may be reproduced, distributed, stored, transmitted, or posted in any form by any means without prior written permission.
Editors of the 2017 *Journey of Faith for Children:* Theresa Nienaber-Panuski and Pat Fosarelli, MD, DMin.
Design and production: Wendy Barnes, Lorena Mitre Jimenez, John Krus, and Bill Townsend. Illustration: Jeff Albrecht.
Unless noted, Scripture texts in this work are taken from the *New American Bible,* revised edition © 2000, 1991, 1986, 1970 Confraternity of Christian Doctrine, Washington, D.C., and are used by permission of the copyright owner. All Rights Reserved. No part of the *New American Bible* may be reproduced in any form without permission in writing from the copyright owner. Excerpts from the English translation of the *Catechism of the Catholic Church* for the United States of America © 1994 United States Catholic Conference, Inc.—*Libreria Editrice Vaticana;* English translation of the *Catechism of the Catholic Church: Modifications from the Editio Typica* © 1997 United States Catholic Conference, Inc.—*Libreria Editrice Vaticana.* Compliant with *The Roman Missal, Third Edition.*
Printed in the United States of America. 21 20 19 18 17 / 5 4 3 2 1. Third Edition.

Liguori
PUBLICATIONS
A Redemptorist Ministry

Closing Prayer

Ask the children to sit in a comfortable position and reflect upon the words of 1 Samuel 3:7–10 either in song or spoken word.

Take-Home

Ask the children to write down the names of any priests or deacons that serve your parish to bring home and share with their parents. Then encourage the children and their parents to say a special prayer for your parish's priests and deacons each day this week.

C10: The People of God

Catechism: 56–64, 121–23, 128–30, 1961–64

Objectives

- Define the Old and New Testaments as key records in our salvation history.
- Define the New Testament as the continuation of the Old Testament.
- Discover that we share a common history with our ancestors in faith.

Leader Meditation

Genesis 15—21, 24—46;
Exodus 7—16

Throughout the Old Testament, we see God's constant presence with and protection of the people. We also see the people's constant struggle between faith and fear, between faithfulness to the Lord and the desire for earthly treasure. What do these Scripture passages tell you about God? About God's faithfulness? How do these passages connect you with God's people throughout history?

Leader Preparation

- Read the lesson, this lesson plan, the Scripture passage, and the *Catechism* sections.
- You should also familiarize yourself with the Old Testament stories this lesson covers: Abraham and Sarah, Joseph and the Pharaoh in Egypt, Moses leading the Israelites out of Egypt, Moses and the Ten Commandments, King David, King Solomon, and the prophet John the Baptist.
- Be familiar with this vocabulary word: plagues. It's defined in this guide's glossary.

Welcome

Greet the children as they arrive. Check for supplies and immediate needs. Solicit questions or comments about the previous session and/or share new information and findings. Begin promptly.

Opening Scripture

Genesis 15:1—6

Light the candle and read aloud. Before beginning the lesson handout, ask the children how they know God is with them.

> God chose Abraham and made a covenant with him and his descendants. By the covenant God formed his people and revealed his law to them through Moses. Through the prophets, he prepared them to accept the salvation destined for all humanity.
>
> *CCC 72*

Journey of Faith

The People of God

"So is Peter like the Church's great-great-great-great grandfather?" Tomás asked.

"Kind of," Mrs. Evans said with a smile. "Church history is like a family tree. We can even trace our roots back before Jesus was born! We call it our salvation history. Our ancestors in faith have helped shape a lot of the traditions we have today. We can read about them in the Bible."

CCC 56–64, 121–23, 128–30, 1961–6

The People of God

Give the children time to answer the reflection question. Then ask volunteers to share their responses.

Depending on the average age of children in your group, you may want to read the Scripture passages directly from the Bible, or exclusively use the summarized version in the lesson handout. You know your group best, so use whatever works best! If you want a more active version of this session, you can bring dress-up supplies, divide the children into groups, and ask each group to act out one of these biblical accounts.

Abraham and Sarah

As you read this story, ask the children what sacrament requires them to take a new name. *Confirmation.*

Refer back to your discussion of confirmation as you discuss the importance of taking on a new name. In confirmation, the children will become adults in the Church and will be given the mission to go out and spread God's word. Abraham and Sarah were also given a special mission by God: to go out and grow faith in God.

Answer the reflection question as a group.

Suggested responses include: God always keeps his promises to us, God's word is true, we can always believe God, and so on.

Isaac and Rebekah

As you read this section, remind children of what they learned about the sacraments of the holy Eucharist and penance.

Ask the children how Jesus feeds us.

Through his Body and Blood

Then ask how we can be forgiven when we sin.

By going to the sacrament of penance and reconciliation

Give the children time to answer the reflection question on their own.

What do you want to learn about the history of the Church?

Abraham and Sarah
Genesis 15—21

Abram believed in God when God revealed himself to Abram. When God said, "Abram, take your wife Sarai and go to a place that I will show you," they left their home, friends, and family to follow God. God led them to a place called Canaan and changed their names. Abram became "Abraham," which means "father of many nations." Sarai became "Sarah," which means "princess of the people."

God promised that Abraham would have more children and grandchildren than there were stars in the sky or grains of sand on the shore. Sarah and Abraham were happy, but they were old and didn't have any children. How could God's promise come true?

At last, a son was born, and they named him Isaac.

How do you think God's promise to Abraham came true?

Isaac and Rebekah
Genesis 24—46

Isaac grew up and married Rebekah. They had twin boys named Jacob and Esau.

God changed Jacob's name to Israel. Israel then had twelve sons (Abraham's great-grandsons). The sons of Israel were the beginning of Abraham's many nations.

Jacob's son Joseph had dreams about his brothers bowing down to him. When he told his brothers about his dreams, they were jealous. They plotted to get rid of Joseph and sold him into slavery. But Joseph became a slave to the Pharaoh in Egypt. The Pharaoh liked Joseph so much he made him his second in command.

Back home, Joseph's family was starving. The brothers went to Egypt and begged the Pharaoh for food. They didn't recognize Joseph, but he knew who they were. Joseph wasn't angry. He loved his brothers and forgave them. He told his brothers to bring their father to Egypt. His family stayed in Egypt and lived with Joseph for many years.

Why do you think Joseph forgave his brothers?

Moses
Book of Exodus

The twelve families of Israel grew and were called the Israelites. After many years, a new Pharaoh began to worry that there were too many Israelites. The Pharaoh made them slaves and had their sons killed at birth. One mother hid her son in a basket and put it in a river. The Pharaoh's daughter found the baby and named him Moses. She raised Moses as her son. But when Moses grew up, he got into trouble and ran away.

God told Moses to return to Egypt and tell the Pharaoh to free the Israelites. Moses was afraid because the Pharaoh was powerful. So God let him bring his brother Aaron with him. When the Pharaoh said no, God sent ten **plagues**, things that brought trouble to the Egyptians, until the Israelites could finally leave (Exodus 7—12).

Then God parted the sea so the Israelites could pass through safely (Exodus 14) and sent them manna, or bread, from heaven to eat on their journey (Exodus 16).

How does God continue to protect Abraham's descendants?

What other "bread from heaven" has God sent us?

The Road to Freedom

After God's people left Egypt, they traveled in the desert for forty years! They were tired and hungry and sometimes they lost faith in God. They complained to Moses a lot. But God stayed with them and took care of them until they reached the Promised Land. You can read more about their journey in Exodus, Numbers, and Deuteronomy.

David
1 Samuel 16—17

Samuel was a prophet. One day, God told Samuel to anoint a king for his people. God sent him to Jesse, a man in Bethlehem who had eight sons. David was the youngest son, a shepherd boy. When Samuel saw him, God said, "There—anoint him, for this is the one!" (16:12).

When the Israelites were at war with the Philistines, a tall, strong Philistine named Goliath bragged that he could defeat anyone. David was brave and agreed to fight him. All David had were five stones and a slingshot. He didn't even have armor! But David had God. God worked through David to do something great! David hit Goliath on the head using his slingshot and won the battle.

What does the story of David teach us about God's view of power and kingship?

Where else does God show us this view of power and kingship?

Moses

The Exodus account given here is a very condensed version. If you have time, you may want to read excerpts from the Bible to give more details.

Answer the reflection questions as a group.

Suggested responses include: God saved the Israelites from the Egyptians, God parted the Red Sea for the Israelites to cross safely, God made sure the Israelites had food and water in the desert, and so on.

God gives us "bread from heaven" in the form of his Body in the Eucharist.

David

Answer the reflection questions as a group.

God believes being strong, rich, and powerful on earth aren't necessarily important traits for a king. God wants his people to be humble and to rely on him for their power.

God shows us this type of kingship in the New Testament. Jesus is the king of heaven and earth, but he comes to earth small and humble, not strong and powerful.

Final Activity

Give the children time to complete the activity. The answers are below.

Abraham	Father of Israelites
Moses	Led the Israelites out of Egypt
David	Great king
Aaron	Brother of Moses
Sarah	Mother of Isaac
Joseph	Sold into slavery
Rebekah	Wife of Isaac

WHO'S WHO IN THE OLD TESTAMENT

Match the name of the biblical person in the left column to his or her role in the right column.

Abraham	Sold into slavery
Moses	Mother of Isaac
David	Brother of Moses
Aaron	Wife of Isaac
Sarah	Led the Israelites out of Egypt
Joseph	Father of Israelites
Rebekah	Great king

In Short

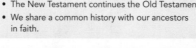

- The Old and New Testaments record key events of our salvation history.
- The New Testament continues the Old Testament.
- We share a common history with our ancestors in faith.

Journey of Faith for Children, Catechumenate, C10 (826344)

Imprimi Potest: Stephen T. Rehrauer, CSsR, Provincial, Denver Province, the Redemptorists.

Imprimatur: "In accordance with CIC 827, permission to publish has been granted on May 3, 2017, by Bishop Mark S. Rivituso, Vicar General, Archdiocese of St. Louis. Permission to publish is an indication that nothing contrary to Church teaching is contained in this work. It does not imply any endorsement of the opinions expressed in the publication, nor is any liability assumed by this permission."

Journey of Faith © 2000, 2017 Liguori Publications, Liguori, MO 63057. To order, visit Liguori.org or call 800-325-9521. Liguori Publications, a nonprofit corporation, is an apostolate of the Redemptorists. To learn more about the Redemptorists, visit Redemptorists.com. All rights reserved. No part of this publication may be reproduced, distributed, stored, transmitted, or posted in any form by any means without prior written permission.

Editors of the 2017 *Journey of Faith for Children*: Theresa Nienaber-Panuski and Pat Fosarelli, MD, DMin.

Design and production: Wendy Barnes, Lorena Mitre Jimenez, John Krus, and Bill Townsend. Illustration: Jeff Albrecht.

Unless noted, Scripture texts in this work are taken from the *New American Bible*, revised edition © 2000, 1991, 1986, 1970 Confraternity of Christian Doctrine, Washington, D.C., and are used by permission of the copyright owner. All Rights Reserved. No part of the *New American Bible* may be reproduced in any form without permission in writing from the copyright owner. Excerpts from the English translation of the *Catechism of the Catholic Church for the United States of America* © 1994 United States Catholic Conference, Inc.—Libreria Editrice Vaticana; English translation of the *Catechism of the Catholic Church: Modifications from the Editio Typica* © 1997 United States Catholic Conference, Inc.—Libreria Editrice Vaticana. Compliant with *The Roman Missal, Third Edition.*

Printed in the United States of America. 21 20 19 18 17 / 5 4 3 2 1. Third Edition.

Liguori
PUBLICATIONS
A Redemptorist Ministry

Closing Prayer

Ask for special intentions, then pray the Our Father and the Glory Be together as a closing prayer.

Take-Home

To help the children get more familiar with the Bible, ask them to look through the Old Testament (with the help of an adult) for an account of God's Chosen People not covered in today's session. Ask the children to write down the Bible citation for the story to share at the beginning of your next session.

C11: The Early Church

Catechism: 425, 748–76, 858

Objectives

- Begin to outline how the Catholic Church developed over time.
- Identify Sts. Peter and Paul as leaders of the early Church.
- Discover how Christians in the early Church faced persecution for their beliefs.

Leader Meditation

Matthew 10:5–42

Read and reflect on the mission of the Twelve Apostles. How is the mission of the twelve similar to your own mission as Christ's witness? When have you felt like a sheep among wolves? When have you felt comforted by Christ's words, "Even the hairs of your head are all counted. So do not be afraid"?

Leader Preparation

- Read the lesson, this lesson plan, the Scripture passage, and the *Catechism* sections.
- Prepare copies of the Apostles' Creed to use as the closing prayer (ideally one copy for each child).
- Be familiar with the following vocabulary terms: Pentecost, Roman Empire, persecute. The definitions are in this guide's glossary.

Welcome

Greet the children as they arrive. Check for supplies and immediate needs. Solicit questions or comments about the previous session and/or share new information and findings. Begin promptly.

Opening Scripture

Matthew 10:5–25

Light the candle and read aloud. As a group, make a list of all the things the apostles were commanded to go out and do.

Preach to the lost sheep of Israel (not the pagans or Samaritans), cure the sick, raise the dead, cleanse lepers, drive out demons, do not take payment, and so on.

> The apostles' ministry is the continuation of [Jesus'] mission; Jesus said to the Twelve: "he who receives you receives me."
>
> CCC 858

The Early Church

Tanya raised her hand. "When do we get to hear about Jesus and the apostles? Didn't the Church start with them?" she asked.

"Yeah!" called out Terrence. "I thought the Israelites were Jewish. What does being Jewish have to do with being Christian?"

CCC 425, 748–76, 858

The Early Church

As a group, make a list of all the things the Israelites and the early Church had in common. Refer back to lesson C10 for some examples.

They were both followers of God, they both were given a special mission by God, they both followed a covenant given to them by God, they both had special traditions they practiced to honor God, and so on.

Jesus Makes a Promise

Give the children time to answer the first reflection question on their own.

Answer the second question by making a list as a group.

The children can share their lesson handouts with their parents after each session, the children can lead prayers before family meals, they can share their favorite Bible stories or saint stories with their friends, and so on.

As you finish this section, give the children time to answer the final reflection question. Ask for volunteers to share their responses. This is a good question to share your answer, too!

 What do you think the Israelites and the early Church had in common?

Jesus the Jew

Mary and Joseph were descendants of King David. This means they were Jewish. Jesus was raised Jewish, too. He practiced the Jewish law and celebrated religious feasts with his community. But Jesus knew God had more planned for his people.

Jesus Makes a Promise

Jesus came to fulfill God's kingdom. He looked for people who would follow him and believe in him. Jesus chose twelve disciples (the apostles) and taught them. For years, Jesus stayed with his apostles, walked and ate with them, and showed them many things. When it was time for Jesus to leave this world, he sent the apostles to preach and teach. Jesus promised them a Helper:

> *"When he comes, the Spirit of truth, he will guide you to all truth. He will not speak on his own, but he will speak what he hears, and will declare to you the things that are coming. He will glorify me, because he will take from what is mine and declare it to you. Everything that the Father has is mine."*
>
> John 16:13–15

Jesus shared his Spirit with the apostles and assured them they could lead the world to the truth. All baptized Christians are asked to take part in this mission.

 How would you feel if you were one of the apostles and had to spread the good news?

How can you share what you are learning about in RCIA with your friends and family?

After Jesus died, his apostles were sad and scared. Instead of preaching and teaching, they hid behind locked doors. They didn't want to be hurt or killed like Jesus.

But Jesus came back! He appeared to his disciples many times. He spoke with them and ate with them again. They were very happy! They finally understood that Jesus could never die. Once again, Jesus promised to send the Holy Spirit to help them. Then he ascended to heaven.

 How would you feel if Jesus came to talk and eat with you?

The Birthday of the Church
Acts 2

The disciples were praying in an upstairs room. They didn't know how they were going to build Jesus' Church. They needed help.

Suddenly a roaring sound, like a strong wind, filled the house. The Holy Spirit came, looking like a flame, and rested over their heads. The Holy Spirit gave the apostles the courage to speak for Jesus. They went outside and started preaching. Hundreds of thousands believed in Jesus' Word and joined the Church.

We celebrate this day, called **Pentecost**, as the birthday of the Church.

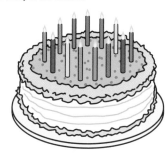

A Man Named Saul

Being a Christian in the early Church was dangerous. Anywhere the apostles tried to preach or the early Church tried to grow, the **Roman Empire** would **persecute** Christians. That meant they would arrest, hurt, or kill Christians just because they were Christians.

There was a Jewish man named Saul who was really mean to Christians. He would go to their houses and drag them off to prison. All the Christians were afraid of Saul.

One day, Saul was heading out to arrest more Christians:

> "A light from the sky suddenly flashed around him. He fell to the ground and heard a voice saying to him, 'Saul, Saul, why are you persecuting me?' He said, 'Who are you, sir?' The reply came, 'I am Jesus, whom you are persecuting. Now get up and go into the city and you will be told what you must do.'"
>
> Acts 9:3–6

The men traveling with Saul also heard the voice. But they didn't see anyone. When Saul got up, he couldn't see. The men he was with had to lead him down the road.

Next, God sent a man named Ananias to Saul. Ananias knew everything Saul had done. He didn't want to go. But God told him, "Go, for this man is a chosen instrument of mine to carry my name…" (Acts 9:15). Through God's power, Ananias healed Saul. God changed Saul's name to Paul. Paul became one of the greatest preachers the Church ever had. His writings, along with the Gospels, make up most of the New Testament.

The Birthday of the Church

As you discuss Pentecost, remind the children that Pentecost occurs fifty days after Easter. If you have a liturgical calendar in your room, circle Pentecost Sunday and tell the children the day on which it will be celebrated this year. If your parish does anything special for Pentecost—like encouraging all parishioners to wear red to Mass— explain those traditions.

Emphasize that the Holy Spirit, the Advocate Jesus promised us, will come to children in a special way when they are confirmed.

Their confirmation will mark their full initiation into the Church community and, like the apostles, it will mean they have been given a mission of evangelization, to go and share the good news.

A Man Named Saul

Depending on the average age of the children in your group, you may want to read all or part of Saul's conversion story from the Bible rather than the lesson adaption. This account can be found in Acts 9:1–30.

As you discuss Saul's story, ask the children if they can think of any other holy people who didn't start out holy. The children should have some examples as they research for their confirmation or baptismal name, but you may want to prompt them with the names and brief stories of some saints with similar histories.

Here are two examples to get you started. Saint Augustine of Hippo spent most of his youth engaging in bad behavior and living as a pagan until he finally converted to Christianity. As a teenager, Teresa of Ávila cared more about boys and clothes than God, but after spending time in a convent, she began to learn more about God and change her life.

Final Activity

As you wrap up your lesson, give the children time to complete the final activity. If they're stuck on a word, encourage them to look back through the lesson handout for help. Walk around as the children work, affirming correct answers and clarifying any confusion. Answers are provided below.

1. Jesus called twelve <u>apostles</u> and prepared them for the ministry of <u>preaching</u>.

2. On <u>Pentecost</u>, Jesus sent the <u>Advocate</u> to the upper room.

3. <u>Paul</u> was blind but then was healed by <u>Ananias</u>.

4. Before the <u>ascension</u>, Jesus <u>promised</u> to send the Spirit.

FILL IN THE BLANK

Complete the following sentences by selecting a word beginning with A and with P from the lists below.

A List

Advocate

Ananias

Apostles

Ascension

P List

Paul

Pentecost

Preaching

Promised

Jesus called twelve _____ and prepared them for the

ministry of _____ .

On _____ , Jesus sent the _____ to

the upper room.

_____ was blind, but then was healed

by _____ .

Before the _____ , Jesus _____ to

send the Spirit.

In Short

- The Christian Church developed over time.
- Saints Peter and Paul led the early Church.
- Christians in the early Church faced persecution.

Journey of Faith for Children, Catechumenate, C11 (826344)
Imprimi Potest: Stephen T. Rehrauer, CSsR, Provincial, Denver Province, the Redemptorists.
Imprimatur: "In accordance with CIC 827, permission to publish has been granted on May 3, 2017, by Bishop Mark S. Rivituso, Vicar General, Archdiocese of St. Louis. Permission to publish is an indication that nothing contrary to Church teaching is contained in this work. It does not imply any endorsement of the opinions expressed in the publication, nor is any liability assumed by this permission."
Journey of Faith © 2000, 2017 Liguori Publications, Liguori, MO 63057. To order, visit Liguori.org or call 800-325-9521. Liguori Publications, a nonprofit corporation, is an apostolate of the Redemptorists. To learn more about the Redemptorists, visit Redemptorists.com. All rights reserved. No part of this publication may be reproduced, distributed, stored, transmitted, or posted in any form by any means without prior written permission.
Editors of the 2017 *Journey of Faith for Children:* Theresa Nienaber-Panuski and Pat Fosarelli, MD, DMin.
Design and production: Wendy Barnes, Lorena Mitre Jimenez, John Krus, and Bill Townsend. Illustration: Jeff Albrecht.
Unless noted, Scripture texts in this work are taken from the *New American Bible*, revised edition © 2000, 1991, 1986, 1970 Confraternity of Christian Doctrine, Washington, D.C., and are used by permission of the copyright owner. All Rights Reserved. No part of the *New American Bible* may be reproduced in any form without permission in writing from the copyright owner. Excerpts from the English translation of the *Catechism of the Catholic Church for the United States of America* © 1994 United States Catholic Conference, Inc.—*Libreria Editrice Vaticana;* English translation of the *Catechism of the Catholic Church: Modifications from the Editio Typica* © 1997 United States Catholic Conference, Inc.—*Libreria Editrice Vaticana.* Compliant with *The Roman Missal, Third Edition.*
Printed in the United States of America. 21 20 19 18 17 / 5 4 3 2 1. Third Edition.

Liguori
PUBLICATIONS
A Redemptorist Ministry

Closing Prayer

Read the Apostles' Creed as a closing prayer. If you have only one copy of the Creed, you may wish to pass it around the group, allowing volunteers to each read a few lines and then pass it on, or read each line and ask the children to repeat it after you.

Take-Home

At home, ask the children and their families to compose a special family prayer to the Holy Spirit and pray that prayer together each day this week either in the morning before starting the day or in the evening before bed.

C12: Church History

Catechism: 811–70

Objectives

- Begin to outline major historic events in Church history.
- Discover some of the saints or religious orders that helped shape the Church.
- Identify the Holy Spirit as the guiding force of the Church.

Leader Meditation

Matthew 28:16–20

With these words from Matthew, Jesus breathed life into his Church. The same words still hold us together today, giving life to the Church. Hear Jesus saying these words to you. Share this amazing truth with each participant in your RCIA class today. The Lord who leads the Church promises to be with each one of us every day.

Leader Preparation

- Read the lesson, this lesson plan, the Scripture passage, and the *Catechism* sections.
- If you have anyone in your parish who is a missionary or who belongs to a religious order, invite them to come speak about their work and how it helps grow the Church.
- Be familiar with the following vocabulary terms: Constantine the Great, Church Fathers, schism, Eastern Orthodox Church, Constantinople, Western (Latin) Church, Martin Luther, Protestant, religious orders, missionaries, Vatican II. The definitions are in this guide's glossary.

Welcome

Greet the children as they arrive. Check for supplies and immediate needs. Solicit questions or comments about the previous session and/or share new information and findings. Begin promptly.

Opening Scripture

Matthew 28:16–20

Light the candle and read aloud. After the reading, ask the children what command Jesus gave his apostles. *(To make disciples of all nations, baptize them, and teach them as Jesus did.)* Then ask the children if they think this command was just for the apostles, or if all Christians have a mission to spread Jesus' teachings. *(All Christians have a mission to evangelize, but the apostles were called to do this in a special way, as priests.)*

> The Church, endowed with the gifts of her founder and faithfully observing his precepts of charity, humility and self-denial, receives the mission of proclaiming and establishing among all peoples the Kingdom of Christ and of God, and she is on earth the seed and the beginning of that kingdom.
>
> *CCC 768*

Church History

"Who can tell me one thing that was passed down from your grandparents, to your parents, to you?" Mrs. Evans asked.

"My gramps always made a big Sunday dinner for the family. Now my dad does it. When I'm grown up, I'll be the one who has the family over," Terrence said with a smile.

"My mom wore my grandma's wedding dress," Lisa added. "My mom says she's saving it for me if I ever want it."

"Great!" Mrs. Evans said, encouragingly. "Our family in faith has traditions like that, too. These traditions have been passed on for generations, and Catholics all over the world share them."

CCC 811–70

Church History

Give the children time to answer the reflection question by listing some of their family's traditions. To get the children started, share some traditions of your own.

History: A Family Story

Give the children time to answer the reflection question and invite volunteers to share.

Answer the second reflection question in this section as a group. You may prompt responses by asking the children why it's important for them to learn about the faith from someone like you before becoming Catholic, or why it's important for that person to have a sponsor or godparent to help him or her live the faith.

Responses may vary, but the children should come to an understanding that, just like in school, it's important to learn about the faith from someone who is an expert in the subject so you know what you're learning is correct. It's also important to learn all about the traditions of the Church from someone who is part of it. Our family traditions may seem odd or be misunderstood by someone who has never taken part in them or who doesn't know their history.

Family Separations

As you discuss the schisms that led to separations in the early Church, ask the children if they've ever gotten into an argument with a friend only to realize later it was a misunderstanding or someone had interpreted a word or action the wrong way. This is kind of like what led to the disagreements in the early Church.

As you discuss a very abbreviated version of the Protestant Reformation, be sensitive to those children coming from a Protestant background. While we disagree with these churches on some points of theology, emphasize that we all share one baptism and one God. Being Protestant does not make someone a bad person. In fact, finding out what beliefs we have in common is a great starting point for talking about what makes the Catholic Church different.

 What traditions have been passed down in your family?

 List the hobbies or interests you share with at least one other person in your family.

History: A Family Story

Every family has a story and a history. Knowing what happened in your family before you were born can help you understand your family, and yourself, better. If your great-great grandfather was a pioneer, it might explain why you like to explore new places. If your grandmother made clothes for people, you might understand your love of clothing.

The history of the Church has many stages. Learning more about the Church will help you better understand your religion. It may even help you understand yourself!

 In the 300s, under the Roman ruler **Constantine the Great**, the Roman Empire allowed Christianity legally. This made it possible to gather, worship, and study Jesus' teachings in peace. As the Church began to grow, **Church Fathers**, very knowledgeable and faithful bishops and monks, helped the people understand their faith. Some of these early Church Fathers include Sts. Ignatius, Clement, Ambrose, Jerome, Basil, Gregory, and Augustine.

Why was it important for new Catholics to learn about the faith from people like the Church Fathers?

Family Separations

Even with the Holy Spirit to guide us, we can still make mistakes. When parts of the Church disagree and separate, we call it a **schism**, which means a split or division. Sometimes people get mixed-up and think their truth is God's truth. Over time, mixed-up thinking led to arguments within the Church. Some people even left the Church completely because of these disagreements. God still wants everyone in his family to be together. So even today the Church is working to become one again.

In 1054, the **Eastern**, or **Orthodox**, Church in **Constantinople** (now Istanbul, Turkey) didn't agree with the pope's role or how the Church talked about the Holy Spirit. So it separated from the **Western**, or **Latin**, Church in Rome.

During the 1500s, a Catholic monk named **Martin Luther** and others saw mistakes being made. He wanted the Church to change its ways. Luther didn't want to start a whole new church. But there was a lot of miscommunication. Then nonreligious leaders got involved and confused things even more! All this confusion led to Luther and others breaking away from the Church to form churches of their own. These newly created churches were called **Protestant** because they were created as a result of people protesting what was going on in the Church at the time.

Family Expansions

Some Catholic groups created religious orders. **Religious orders** are groups of men and women who live together and focus on a specific spirituality or way of serving God. Some religious orders today are the Jesuits, Franciscans, Redemptorists, and Dominicans. They teach in schools, help in hospitals, preach to people, and live lives of prayer.

Others choose to be missionaries. **Missionaries** go into distant parts of the world to spread the Good News and serve the poor. Many missionary communities are still active today.

The Twentieth-Century Church

In 1959, Pope St. John XXIII called together Catholic bishops, laypeople, and leaders from other Christian communities for a meeting known as the Second Vatican Council, or **Vatican II**. This meeting resulted in important messages like:

- Laypeople should become more involved in the Church's work and assist priests during Mass by proclaiming the first and second readings, leading songs, and planning Church celebrations.

- Mass could be celebrated in the languages of the people (like English) and not just Latin.

- People were encouraged to study the Bible and spend more time learning about their faith.

- The Church family would continue to help the needy, promote education, and fight greed.

- Even though there have been disagreements in the past, the Church would work with other religions and nonreligious people to end bad things like abortion, war, and poverty in the world.

The Church Today

The Church works hard to preserve the truth. The world has changed a lot since Jesus lived, but our God and our faith remains the same:

- God the Father is Creator.

- God the Son saved us and gave us the sacraments, especially the Eucharist.

- God the Holy Spirit always guides the Church, through good times and bad.

- The Church still inspires people through God's word in Scripture.

Family Expansions

As you discuss religious orders, ask the children if they know anyone living in a religious order or if they know any missionaries. If you have anyone in your parish who has done missionary work, or someone who is a brother or sister in a religious order, ask them to lead this section by sharing their experience.

The Twentieth-Century Church

As you discuss Vatican II, emphasize that popes in the Church often write and present documents that expand on our understanding of the Church or that put Church teaching in the context of our world today. This doesn't mean that the pope is changing Church teaching. Core teachings of the Church have always remained the same. It is the pope's job to clarify those teachings when people feel lost, and to remind people how we can live those teachings today.

The Church Today

As you read through the bulleted list, invite the children to respond, "I believe it!" after each item.

C12

Final Activity

As you wrap up today's lesson, give the children time to complete the final activity on their own or with a partner. If the children want a challenge, encourage them to go through the lesson and add terms to each column that aren't listed in their word bank, or words that aren't even covered in their handout. If you have time, draw or display the chart on the board and ask the children to fill it in with their answers. The answers are below. Possible bonus words appear in italics.

WHO'S WHO AND WHAT'S WHAT?

Determine whether each word below is a person, religious order, Christian church, or an event in Church history. Write it in the correct column.

Ambrose   Constantine   Council   Franciscans

Jesuits   Lutherans   Orthodox   Schism

People	Orders / Groups	Churches	Events

In Short

- The Church has a varied and rich history.
- Saints and religious orders helped shape the Church.
- The Holy Spirit guides the Church.

Journey of Faith for Children, Catechumenate, C12 (826344)
Imprimi Potest: Stephen T. Rehrauer, CSsR, Provincial, Denver Province, the Redemptorists.
Imprimatur: "In accordance with CIC 827, permission to publish has been granted on May 3, 2017, by Bishop Mark S. Rivituso, Vicar General, Archdiocese of St. Louis. Permission to publish is an indication that nothing contrary to Church teaching is contained in this work. It does not imply any endorsement of the opinions expressed in the publication, nor is any liability assumed by this permission."
Journey of Faith © 2000, 2017 Liguori Publications, Liguori, MO 63057. To order, visit Liguori.org or call 800-325-9521. Liguori Publications, a nonprofit corporation, is an apostolate of the Redemptorists. To learn more about the Redemptorists, visit Redemptorists.com. All rights reserved. No part of this publication may be reproduced, distributed, stored, transmitted, or posted in any form by any means without prior written permission.
Editors of the 2017 *Journey of Faith for Children:* Theresa Nienaber-Panuski and Pat Fosarelli, MD, DMin.
Design and production: Wendy Barnes, Lorena Mitre Jimenez, John Krus, and Bill Townsend. Illustration: Jeff Albrecht.
Unless noted, Scripture texts in this work are taken from the *New American Bible*, revised edition © 2000, 1991, 1986, 1970 Confraternity of Christian Doctrine, Washington, D.C., and are used by permission of the copyright owner. All Rights Reserved. No part of the *New American Bible* may be reproduced in any form without permission in writing from the copyright owner. Excerpts from the English translation of the *Catechism of the Catholic Church for the United States of America* © 1994 United States Catholic Conference, Inc.—Libreria Editrice Vaticana; English translation of the *Catechism of the Catholic Church: Modifications from the Editio Typica* © 1997 United States Catholic Conference, Inc.—Libreria Editrice Vaticana.
Compliant with *The Roman Missal, Third Edition.*
Printed in the United States of America. 21 20 19 18 17 / 5 4 3 2 1. Third Edition.

Liguori PUBLICATIONS
A Redemptorist Ministry

PEOPLE	ORDERS / GROUPS	CHURCHES	EVENTS
Ambrose	Franciscans	Lutherans	Schism
Jesus	Jesuits	Orthodox or *Eastern*	Council
Pope St. John XXIII	*Missionaries*	*Western* or *Latin*	*Vatican II*
Martin Luther	*Dominicans*		
St. Gregory	*Redemptorists*		
St. Augustine			
St. Ignatius			
Constantine			

Closing Prayer

Pray the Our Father together. Remind the children that this prayer has been with the Church throughout its history and is still prayed in many Christian denominations today.

Take-Home

Encourage children to pick one of the people, groups, churches, or events from the final activity to do more research on this week with their parents, godparents, or sponsor.

C13: Living Like Jesus Today

Catechism: 1776–1832

Objectives

- Identify Jesus as our example for living the ideal, moral life.
- Discover that our conscience is something we have to form as we grow.
- Begin to practice self-reflection or an examination of conscience.

Leader Meditation

Proverbs 3:5–6

It can be easy for us to look at other people and think, "Well, at least I'm not doing that." But when we "trust in the LORD," we have to do more than rely on our own interpretations of right and wrong. We have to interpret the world the way Jesus sees us. It's often the most difficult situations and the hardest choices that require us to rely on ourselves the least and God the most. When have you needed the Church to help you make difficult choices? Has it been hard to follow the Church's teaching in these moments?

Leader Preparation

- Read the lesson, this lesson plan, the Scripture passage, and the *Catechism* sections.
- You may also want to have the Ten Commandments visible somewhere in the room for this lesson or have your Bible open to Exodus 20:1–17.
- Print out each commandment on its own sheet of paper for the final activity. If you plan to have children complete the activity in groups, print out enough sets for each group.
- Consider using the song "Restless" (Audrey Assad and Matt Maher, from *The House You're Building*, Sparrow) as your closing prayer.
- Be familiar with the following vocabulary terms: Ten Commandments, conscience. The definitions are in this guide's glossary.

Welcome

Greet the children as they arrive. Check for supplies and immediate needs. Solicit questions or comments about the previous session and/or share new information and findings. Begin promptly.

Opening Scripture

Matthew 22:34–40

Light the candle and read aloud. Ask the children if they think there's a difference between just following the rules because you have to and following the rules because you understand them and know it's the right thing to do. This might be tough for the children to understand, so try to offer some examples, such as the difference between not talking in class because you just don't want to get in trouble and not talking in class because you want to learn.

> The Ten Commandments are engraved by God in the human heart.
>
> *CCC 2072*

Living Like Jesus Today

Lisa was speaking to the class. "One of my friends at soccer says that Catholics have too many rules and her religion doesn't. Mrs. Evans, why do Catholics like rules?"

Mrs. Evans smiled. "Some people do think we have a lot of rules. But most of them are the same as other Christians have because they're based on what Jesus said or what's in the Bible. And just like rules at home and in school, they make our lives better. Let's take the Ten Commandments."

CCC 1776–1832

The Ten Commandments

To help emphasize that obeying the Ten Commandments isn't just about not getting in trouble with God, as you go through each of the commandments create a corresponding "do" or "will" command that goes with it. An example for each of the commandments has been given below, but your class might come up with different ones.

1. You will show God you love him as your heavenly Father.

2. You will treat God's name with respect like you treat the names of the other people you love.

3. You will celebrate your faith in a special way by participating in the Mass (at least) every Sunday.

4. You will use Jesus as your example of how to treat your parents and other adults.

5. You will respect life in every form.

6. You will keep the sacraments, especially marriage, holy.

7. You will work honestly for all you have, and share it with those in need.

8. You will tell the truth and avoid gossiping or making up stories.

9. You will respect other people's possessions.

10. You will treat everyone as a member of the body of Christ; we are all family in Jesus!

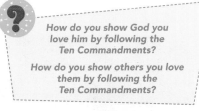

The Ten Commandments

The **Ten Commandments** are the rules God gave Moses in the Old Testament. These ten rules explain how God wants us to live. The first three tell us how to love God. The other seven tell us how to love each other.

1. You will not worship anything or anyone but God.

2. You will only use God's name with respect.

3. You will keep Sunday, God's day, holy.

4. You will respect and listen to your father and mother.

5. You will not kill.

6. You will be loyal to your husband or wife.

7. You will not steal.

8. You will not tell lies.

9. You will not be jealous of other people's possessions.

10. You will not be jealous of other people's family members.

Adapted from Exodus 20:1–17

The Two Great Commandments

Jesus was born and raised in the Jewish faith. He knew the Hebrew Scriptures well. He knew the Ten Commandments and the other laws and rules in the Old Testament. But Jesus saw these laws were getting mixed up by some of the Jewish leaders. They were making the laws about *looking* holy, not about loving God and trying to *be* holy. Jesus taught that laws are good, but we have to live laws with our hearts.

Jesus gave us two new commandments to make sure loving God and each other were always at the heart of our laws. (See Matthew 22:37–39, Mark 12:30–31, Luke 10:27)

1. "You shall love the LORD, your God, with your whole heart, and with your whole being, and with your whole strength" (Deuteronomy 6:5).

2. "You shall love your neighbor as yourself" (Leviticus 19:18).

How do you show God you love him by following the Ten Commandments?

How do you show others you love them by following the Ten Commandments?

The Two Great Commandments

As you discuss this section, ask the children why they think it's important we follow both the letter and spirit of God's laws, rather than just follow the rules so we look holy.

It's important that we really believe, and not just want to look like we believe. If we only follow the laws when people can see us, we're more likely to be tempting to sin when no one's around to see us.

Give the children time to answer the two reflection questions on their own and then ask volunteers to share their responses.

If we know and believe in Jesus, it shows in everything we do. We are like mirrors that reflect his ways. We listen to Jesus, learn from Jesus, and follow Jesus' example.

When we live our lives like Jesus, we become stronger. When we put God first, we can stand up to people who want us to do bad or wrong things.

"Everyone who listens to these words of mine and acts on them will be like a wise man who built his house on rock. The rain fell, the floods came, and the winds blew and buffeted the house. But it did not collapse; it had been set solidly on rock."
Matthew 7:24–25

Your Conscience Is Your Guide

How do you know when you are making the right decision? What tells you if something is right or wrong?

Sometimes you know because your parents or other adults you trust have told you. Sometimes Jesus, through the Church, helps to explain why something is right or wrong to us. Our ability to recognize if something is right or wrong, with the help of the Church, trusted adults, and the Holy Spirit, is called **conscience**. Your conscience is the Holy Spirit speaking to your heart, helping you to make the right decisions.

How do you figure out what the right thing to do is?

The Church Helps Us

Jesus told his apostles to pay attention to everything he taught them. Before he went back to heaven, Jesus gave the apostles and the people they would choose to lead after them, the authority to speak and act in his name. The apostles used Jesus' teachings and example to lead the Church.

Today, the pope, bishops, and priests continue the work of the apostles. Jesus and the Holy Spirit guide them. The world has changed a lot since Jesus' time. That's why the pope and the bishops use Jesus' teachings to help us live like Jesus in a different kind of place. The teachings of the pope and the bishops should guide our decisions and remove confusion about what is right and wrong.

And just like Jesus taught us, everything we do should be done with love for God and each other!

Your Conscience Is Your Guide

Answer the reflection question as a group. If you have time, you can even create a group guide to making right decisions by creating a flow chart or step-by-step instructions using children's responses. Be sure to include prayer or asking God as one of your steps.

Encourage children to copy your guide and use it whenever they're faced with a big decision. You can also encourage children to use the guide backward as a guide to reflection on moments where they know they didn't make the right choice but weren't sure what to do. This will help them learn from their experience and provide an introduction to more ambitious forms of prayer, like St. Ignatius' Examen.

The Church Helps Us

As you discuss this section, make a list of all the ways the Church helps us live like Jesus.

We hear how Jesus acts through the Gospel readings at Mass, the Church gives us guidelines for how to live like Jesus, we can participate in the sacrament of penance to have our sins forgiven, we can reflect on the lives of the saints to see how ordinary people became more like Jesus.

Final Activity

As you wrap up the lesson, give the children time to complete the activity on their own. If you'd like a more active variation on this lesson, print out each commandment on its own sheet of paper, shuffle the papers, and ask the children to put them in order. You can make a competition out of it by splitting the children into teams and asking them to compete for the fastest time.

The answers to the activity as written appear below.

8 Don't lie.

7 Don't steal.

2 Don't use God's name in a sloppy or bad way.

3 Keep God's day holy.

6 Be loyal to your spouse.

9 Don't be jealous of other people's stuff.

10 Don't be jealous of other people's family members.

4 Obey your mother and father.

1 Make sure that you don't love anything more than God.

5 Don't kill.

THE TEN COMMANDMENTS, IN ORDER

Put the following commandments in order by writing a number 1–10 on the line next to it.

_____ Don't lie.

_____ Don't steal.

_____ Don't use God's name in a sloppy or bad way.

_____ Keep God's day holy.

_____ Be loyal to your spouse.

_____ Don't be jealous of other people's stuff.

_____ Don't be jealous of other people's family members.

_____ Obey your mother and father.

_____ Make sure that you don't love anything more than God.

_____ Don't kill.

In Short

- Jesus is our example for living a moral life.
- We should reflect on our choices.
- We have to form our conscience.

Journey of Faith for Children, Catechumenate, C13 (826344)

Imprimi Potest: Stephen T. Rehrauer, CSsR, Provincial, Denver Province, the Redemptorists.

Imprimatur: "In accordance with CIC 827, permission to publish has been granted on May 3, 2017, by Bishop Mark S. Rivituso, Vicar General, Archdiocese of St. Louis. Permission to publish is an indication that nothing contrary to Church teaching is contained in this work. It does not imply any endorsement of the opinions expressed in the publication, nor is any liability assumed by this permission."

Journey of Faith © 2000, 2017 Liguori Publications, Liguori, MO 63057. To order, visit Liguori.org or call 800-325-9521. Liguori Publications, a nonprofit corporation, is an apostolate of the Redemptorists. To learn more about the Redemptorists, visit Redemptorists.com. All rights reserved. No part of this publication may be reproduced, distributed, stored, transmitted, or posted in any form by any means without prior written permission.

Editors of the 2017 *Journey of Faith for Children:* Theresa Nienaber-Panuski and Pat Fosarelli, MD, DMin.

Design and production: Wendy Barnes, Lorena Mitre Jimenez, John Krus, and Bill Townsend. Illustration: Jeff Albrecht.

Unless noted, Scripture texts in this work are taken from the *New American Bible,* revised edition © 2000, 1991, 1986, 1970 Confraternity of Christian Doctrine, Washington, D.C., and are used by permission of the copyright owner. All Rights Reserved. No part of the *New American Bible* may be reproduced in any form without permission in writing from the copyright owner. Excerpts from the English translation of the *Catechism of the Catholic Church for the United States of America* © 1994 United States Catholic Conference, Inc.—*Libreria Editrice Vaticana;* English translation of the *Catechism of the Catholic Church: Modifications from the Editio Typica* © 1997 United States Catholic Conference, Inc.—*Libreria Editrice Vaticana.* Compliant with *The Roman Missal, Third Edition.*

Printed in the United States of America. 21 20 19 18 17 / 5 4 3 2 1. Third Edition.

Liguori PUBLICATIONS
A Redemptorist Ministry

Closing Prayer

Dim the lights and ask the children to gather in comfortable positions. Keep the candle lit. Play a recording of "Restless" as a closing prayer.

Take-Home

Encourage the children to create a list of how they and their families can live the Ten Commandments at home. They can decorate this list however they'd like and post it on the fridge or anywhere else where everyone will see it.

C14: Caring for All God's Creatures

Catechism: 1807, 2401–49

Objectives

- Recognize the dignity of life is universal for all people.
- Discover the call of Catholics to respect all life.
- Discover how Catholics work to support dignity, justice, and human rights.

Leader Meditation

Luke 10:25–37

Thank God for the people in your life who have been Good Samaritans to you. Think about simple, everyday ways you can be a Good Samaritan to others.

Leader Preparation

- Read the lesson, this lesson plan, the Scripture passage, and the *Catechism* sections.
- Familiarize yourself with any world or national current events that center on the issues of economic or social justice; use these events as examples, as appropriate for the age of children in your group.
- Be familiar with this vocabulary word: prejudiced. It's defined in this guide's glossary.

Welcome

Greet the children as they arrive. Check for supplies and immediate needs. Solicit questions or comments about the previous session and/or share new information and findings. Begin promptly.

Opening Scripture

Luke 10:25–37

Light the candle and read aloud. Ask volunteers to recall a time when someone took the time to help them when they didn't have to.

> Justice is the moral virtue that consists in the constant and firm will to give [our] due to God and neighbor....The just man, often mentioned in the Sacred Scriptures, is distinguished by habitual right thinking and the uprightness of his conduct toward his neighbor.
>
> *CCC 1807*

Caring for All God's Creatures

"What's wrong?" Tomás was worried about Lisa. She'd been really quiet all class and she seemed upset.

"We had new neighbors move in. They're really nice, but they don't speak English very well because they came here from another country. This morning someone put a sign on their lawn that said, 'Go home.' It's not fair! I want to help them but I don't know how. What should I do?"

CCC 1807, 2401–49

Caring for All God's Creatures

Give children time to answer the reflection questions on their own and then answer both questions together as a class. Emphasize the importance of acting like Jesus but also of responding to situations in ways that children will be safe. Some actions are best left to adults or people in positions of authority.

Looking at God's Children

Divide the children into pairs or groups, depending on the size of your class, and give them time to respond to the reflection question together. Once everyone has had a chance to talk, have each child share one thing he or she learned about their partner. Or, depending on your class size and time restraints, ask the children to rotate partners and do the same thing again. You can rotate as many times as you'd like and, if sponsors and godparents are in your session today, include them in the mix, too!

Prejudice

Emphasize that prejudice doesn't just have to be about a difference we can see or hear (like skin color or whether someone has an accent). It can also include how much money someone's family has, where that person's family lives, or what kind of job their parents have.

Answer the reflection question as a group. Emphasize that inclusion is more than just letting people do the same things as you, but actively including people in your groups and activities.

? *What do you think Lisa should do?*

What do you think Jesus might tell Lisa to do?

Looking at God's Children

Look around the room right now. Does everyone you see look like you? Do you all like the same things? Eat the same food? Come from the same family?

But you're not totally different either. You all have friends. You all have families. You all need food and shelter to survive. You were all created by God.

We all have things that make us the same and things that make us different. We are all "very good" (Genesis 1:31) the way God sees us. God created us to be part of a community and completely ourselves.

Talk to the person next to you. What do you have in common? What makes you different? List a few of those things here.

_____

_____

_____

Prejudice

God made each of us special. We all have things that make us different. But some people think some things make certain people better than others. They only like people who have the same skin color, speak the same language, or like the same things as they do. When people think this way, we say their thoughts are **prejudiced**.

Prejudice causes a lot of suffering and unhappiness. Imagine you went to school and sat down with your best friends. But then someone came by and said you weren't allowed to play with your friends any more because you had blue eyes and they had brown eyes. Then you find out people with blue eyes aren't allowed to eat lunch until everyone with brown eyes eats. And you have to play on an old playground because the new one is only for brown-eyed people.

YOU'RE NOT WELCOME HERE

If that happened you'd probably feel hurt. You'd probably be angry, too.

? *What are some things you can do to make everyone feel included at school? In your neighborhood?*

Sharing What We Have

One way we're different from other people are the things we have. We might have one friend who has the newest clothes and toys. Another friend always gets to go on vacation. A third friend always wears hand-me-downs.

Sometimes we might feel like having things or enough money to get more things are the most important parts of life. Having what we need is important. We all need clothes. We all need food and shelter. It's even OK to like some of the special things we have. But when we care more about our stuff than God and other people, we aren't living like Jesus.

Loving things more than people hurts God and others. God asks us to take care of the poor. We should share what we have, give away toys and clothing we've outgrown, and put people before stuff at all times. God doesn't care if our electronics are outdated or our shoes aren't brand-new. God loves us for us. So we also should love other people for who they are, not what they have.

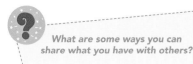

? *What are some ways you can share what you have with others?*

God's World Is in Our Hands

People are the most important part of God's creation, but we have to take care of the rest of God's world, too! God made the world especially for us. That means it's our responsibility to take care of it.

Right after creating the world, God gave Adam the job of naming the animals and caring for the Garden of Eden. Every seed we plant, every tree we water is a gift we give back to God. Every bird we feed, every pet we care for, every animal we protect is both God's gift to us and a living sign of our love and faithfulness toward God.

List three gifts of God's creation that make your life better.

1. _____
2. _____
3. _____

List three things you can do to care for God's creatures and the environment.

1. _____
2. _____
3. _____

Sharing What We Have

Answer the reflection question as a group. If your parish has particular ways it shares with parishioners in need or the larger community—like a parish-run thrift shop, clothing collection bins, or canned-food drives—point those out. If you have boxes or donation bins set up, take a trip with the children to point out where everything is around your parish campus.

God's World Is in Our Hands

Give the children time to complete the reflection questions on their own or with a partner. Then go around the room and ask each child (or pair) to give one thing from each list and collect ideas onto a larger full-group list. If you make this list on poster board or construction paper, ask the children to help you decorate it and then hang it up somewhere around your parish campus so parishioners can see it.

Final Activity

As you wrap up today's lesson, give the children time to complete the activity on their own or with a small group. Walk around as the children work and affirm correct answers and clarify confusion. Answers will vary, but one example has been given to help the children get started.

 LOVING GOD'S CREATION

In the first column, list three ways people hurt others or God's creation. In the second column, list one way we can respond to that hurt. The first one is done for you.

Sin / Hurt	Response
Not letting someone be on your team because he doesn't have the right equipment.	Instead of leaving him out, others on the team could take turns sharing their equipment so everyone can play.
1.	
2.	
3.	

In Short

- The dignity of human life is universal.
- Christians are called to protect human life and respect God's creation.
- Christians are called to support dignity, justice, and the rights for all people.

Journey of Faith for Children, Catechumenate, C14 (826344)
Imprimi Potest: Stephen T. Rehrauer, CSsR, Provincial, Denver Province, the Redemptorists.
Imprimatur: "In accordance with CIC 827, permission to publish has been granted on May 3, 2017, by Bishop Mark S. Rivituso, Vicar General, Archdiocese of St. Louis. Permission to publish is an indication that nothing contrary to Church teaching is contained in this work. It does not imply any endorsement of the opinions expressed in the publication, nor is any liability assumed by this permission."
Journey of Faith © 2000, 2017 Liguori Publications, Liguori, MO 63057. To order, visit Liguori.org or call 800-325-9521. Liguori Publications, a nonprofit corporation, is an apostolate of the Redemptorists. To learn more about the Redemptorists, visit Redemptorists.com. All rights reserved. No part of this publication may be reproduced, distributed, stored, transmitted, or posted in any form by any means without prior written permission.
Editors of the 2017 *Journey of Faith for Children:* Theresa Nienaber-Panuski and Pat Fosarelli, MD, DMin.
Design and production: Wendy Barnes, Lorena Mitre Jimenez, John Krus, and Bill Townsend. Illustration: Jeff Albrecht.
Unless noted, Scripture texts in this work are taken from the *New American Bible*, revised edition © 2000, 1991, 1986, 1970 Confraternity of Christian Doctrine, Washington, D.C., and are used by permission of the copyright owner. All Rights Reserved. No part of the *New American Bible* may be reproduced in any form without permission in writing from the copyright owner. Excerpts from the English translation of the *Catechism of the Catholic Church for the United States of America* © 1994 United States Catholic Conference, Inc.—*Libreria Editrice Vaticana*; English translation of the *Catechism of the Catholic Church: Modifications from the Editio Typica* © 1997 United States Catholic Conference, Inc.—*Libreria Editrice Vaticana*. Compliant with *The Roman Missal, Third Edition.*
Printed in the United States of America. 21 20 19 18 17 / 5 4 3 2 1. Third Edition.

Liguori PUBLICATIONS
A Redemptorist Ministry

Closing Prayer

Ask for a volunteer to read Matthew 5:43–48 as a closing prayer. Here, Jesus asks that we treat everyone, even our enemies, with justice.

Conclude by praying the Our Father together.

Take-Home

With their families, ask the children to make a list of at least three ways family members can sometimes hurt each other and then ways they could act with love instead.

C15: Choose Life Always

Catechism: 1807, 2401–49

Objectives

- Begin to identify some of the modern issues that threaten human life and why they do so.
- Begin to define an intrinsic moral evil and list some actions that fall into this category.
- Discover how Catholics can and do defend life.

Leader Meditation

Genesis 1:24–31

In this passage, the ancient authors speak of God as the author of all life. They proclaim that everything God made is sacred, beautiful, and good. Reflect on the power—and responsibility—inherent in this message.

Leader Preparation

- Read the lesson, this lesson plan, the Scripture passage, and the *Catechism* sections. Because of the topics covered in this lesson, please review the topics covered especially closely. You know the age and maturity of the children in your group best, and you'll know whether more explanation or less detail is needed. Use your discretion in presenting lesson topics to the children in your care today. You may even consider sending a note to parents explaining what will be covered during this lesson.
- Make copies of the closing prayer for each child.
- If your parish has a prolife group, ask a spokesperson—particularly one who is used to speaking with children—to come and talk to your group.
- Be familiar with the following vocabulary terms: abortion, euthanasia, capital punishment, poverty. The definitions are in this guide's glossary.

Welcome

Greet the children as they arrive. Check for supplies and immediate needs. Solicit questions or comments about the previous session and/or share new information and findings. Begin promptly.

Opening Scripture

Genesis 1:24–31

Light the candle and read aloud. Ask the children what this reading tells us about creation. *(That everything is created by God.)* Then ask what God tells humans about the earth. *(God gave the earth to Adam and Eve, and they were called to care for and respect all living things.)*

> Human life is sacred because from its beginning it involves the creative action of God and it remains forever in a special relationship with the Creator, who is its sole end. God alone is the Lord of life from its beginning until its end.
>
> CCC 2258

Choose Life Always

Terrence and Lisa overheard Tanya say she had a volleyball game after RCIA class that night. They wanted to go support Tanya because they knew she was nervous.

Terrence and Lisa stood on the sidelines and jumped and cheered. They screamed, "Go, Tanya!"

Tanya was grateful to have such good friends and that God brought them all together through their RCIA classes.

CCC 1807, 2401–49

Life: The Greatest Gift

Give the children time to complete the reflection question on their own. Then go around the room and ask each child to share one of the things on the list.

Taking Care of God's Gift

Before you start this section, ask the children how they usually treat gifts they get that they really love. Normally you'd take care of a gift, especially if it's something you really love. Emphasize that God gave us the gift of life but people don't always treat it like a gift.

After your discussion of this section, give the children time to answer the reflection question on their own. Ask volunteers to share their response.

Abortion

If you have a spokesperson from your parish prolife group, give the individual time to talk to the children about what they do and how it helps to defend life. You could encourage the speaker to bring a prolife prayer card to share and pray together as a group.

Euthanasia

As you discuss this section, keep the focus on how God has created every life good and for a purpose. Try to keep the focus on why it's important for us to respect life at all stages rather than on the specifics or political aspects surrounding euthanasia.

You may even want to share stories of saints who chose life even when they were very sick or in a lot of pain, or saints who helped others choose life. Some possible saints to cover include Gianna Beretta Molla, Margaret of Castello, Mother Teresa of Calcutta, and Alphonsus Liguori.

Life: The Greatest Gift

God gives us many gifts. Every day, as soon as we wake up, we can begin to count the gifts we receive from God.

List three gifts you received from God today.

1. _____

2. _____

3. _____

When God made the world, he created people in his own image and offers everyone eternal life. That makes human life very special!

Taking Care of God's Gift

When someone gives us a gift, we don't break it or destroy it. We take care of it. We enjoy it. We thank the person for it. God gave us the gift of life. We have to be responsible and take good care of it.

But we don't just take care of our own life. God also calls us to take care of others. When people's lives are in danger, or when people aren't cared for like they should be, we—and all God's people—have to help.

 What are some things you can do to help others?

Abortion

The lives of some children are in danger even before they're born. When a pregnant woman chooses to go to a doctor who will take away her unborn baby's life, it's called **abortion**.

Not everyone is happy when they hear a new baby is coming. Some people get very angry. Some people get very scared. We are called to care both for the new baby and the baby's mother. This is why the Church works to help pregnant females who don't want to be mothers.

 Does your parish have a prolife group? What do they do to help mothers and babies?

Euthanasia

Sometimes people want to end someone's life because that person is very old or very sick. A person may even want to end her or his own life because of age or illness and don't want to suffer. Ending a life because someone does not want to live with an illness or suffering is called **euthanasia**.

People who choose euthanasia often think they are making a good choice. They think they are too old or too sick to ever get better and they don't want to suffer any more. Or their families don't want to see them suffer.

But taking a life away early is never right or good. All humans have dignity, and as part of that dignity all people deserve the right to live life to a natural death. Only God knows best when a life is over. We have to trust that God is looking out for us and our family even when someone is hurting.

Capital Punishment

When someone we love is hurt by another person, we may want to get even or make things right. Some people think that it is an act of justice to punish people who have hurt or killed other people with **capital punishment**. "Capital" means the crime was so serious that the person who did it can be put to death. The Church teaches us that society has a right to defend itself, but if we can be safe without bloodshed, the Church tell us those are the ways we should pursue.

God tells us not to kill but to forgive each other—even many times (Matthew 18:21–22). The Church teaches that because God gives life, only God can take life away. It can be really hard to see good in someone who has done very bad things and hurt other people. The Church reminds us that every person is created in God's image, even people who have done bad things. The Church reminds us that we have to be examples of loving and living like Jesus in the world.

Poverty and Hunger

Many people in the world don't have enough to eat or drink. Some children go to bed hungry every night. It's hard to love life and be thankful when you don't have enough. Not being able to buy the basic things you need to live is called **poverty**. The Church reminds us that it is our responsibility to share what we have with people who need it.

List three things you have that you're grateful for.

1. _____
2. _____
3. _____

List three things you could give away to help someone else.

1. _____
2. _____
3. _____

War

It's not easy for people to agree all the time. Even families argue over little things. When our differences get in the way, life is no longer peaceful and happy. When countries, governments, or other groups fight with each other, it could lead to war.

Many people are hurt and killed during war. Even people who didn't want to go to war. Using weapons and violence is a terrible way to solve problems. It's also a terrible way to treat God's gift of human life. Sometimes war might be necessary, but only when it is the only way to stop people from being hurt or killed. The Church calls us to find other ways to try and solve conflicts first.

List three things you can do to keep peace in your family, school, or neighborhood.

1. _____
2. _____
3. _____

Capital Punishment

As you discuss capital punishment, you may want to discuss with the children the difference between justice and vengeance.

Justice is a virtue that considers what is morally right, and a just decision considers circumstances, reparations, and forgiveness. Vengeance is acting out of hurt and anger to "get even" without considering what a just response might be.

Poverty and Hunger

Give the children time to complete the reflection question on their own or with a partner. Ask volunteers to share one thing from each list.

War

As you discuss, keep the emphasis on cultivating peace rather than the political or violent nature of wars.

Answer the reflection question as a group. Try to list as many ways as you can. You aren't limited to three.

Final Activity

As you wrap up this lesson, give the children time to complete the activity in small groups. Walk around as the children work and affirm correct answers and clarify any confusion. Answers will vary. Sample responses are in red lettering.

Abortion

1. Hold (or donate to) a collection drive of baby supplies to help a mother-to-be in poverty.
2. Offer to play with or share toys with a younger sibling.

HOW CAN I HONOR LIFE?

For each action below, list two things you could do that help or honor life instead.

Abortion

1. _____

2. _____

Euthanasia

1. _____

2. _____

Capital Punishment

1. _____

2. _____

Poverty and Hunger

1. _____

2. _____

War

1. _____

2. _____

In Short

- Some modern issues threaten human life.
- Some actions are evil.
- How Catholics defend life

Journey of Faith for Children, Catechumenate, C15 (826344)

Imprimi Potest: Stephen T. Rehrauer, CSsR, Provincial, Denver Province, the Redemptorists.

Imprimatur: "In accordance with CIC 827, permission to publish has been granted on May 3, 2017, by Bishop Mark S. Rivituso, Vicar General, Archdiocese of St. Louis. Permission to publish is an indication that nothing contrary to Church teaching is contained in this work. It does not imply any endorsement of the opinions expressed in the publication, nor is any liability assumed by this permission."

Journey of Faith © 2000, 2017 Liguori Publications, Liguori, MO 63057. To order, visit Liguori.org or call 800-325-9521. Liguori Publications, a nonprofit corporation, is an apostolate of the Redemptorists. To learn more about the Redemptorists, visit Redemptorists.com. All rights reserved. No part of this publication may be reproduced, distributed, stored, transmitted, or posted in any form by any means without prior written permission.

Editors of the 2017 *Journey of Faith for Children:* Theresa Nienaber-Panuski and Pat Fosarelli, MD, DMin.

Design and production: Wendy Barnes, Lorena Mitre Jimenez, John Krus, and Bill Townsend. Illustration: Jeff Albrecht.

Unless noted, Scripture texts in this work are taken from the *New American Bible,* revised edition © 2000, 1991, 1986, 1970 Confraternity of Christian Doctrine, Washington, D.C., and are used by permission of the copyright owner. All Rights Reserved. No part of the *New American Bible* may be reproduced in any form without permission in writing from the copyright owner. Excerpts from the English translation of the *Catechism of the Catholic Church* for the United States of America © 1994 United States Catholic Conference, Inc.—*Libreria Editrice Vaticana;* English translation of the *Catechism of the Catholic Church: Modifications from the Editio Typica* © 1997 United States Catholic Conference, Inc.—*Libreria Editrice Vaticana.* Compliant with *The Roman Missal, Third Edition.*

Printed in the United States of America. 21 20 19 18 17 / 5 4 3 2 1. Third Edition.

![Liguori Publications logo] Liguori PUBLICATIONS A Redemptorist Ministry

Closing Prayer

Offer today's closing prayer especially for the sick, dying, and unborn. Thank God for the gift of life. Conclude with this adaptation of Bishop Robert Baker's prolife prayer. Ask the children to repeat each line after you.

Lord God,
You are the Protector and
Defender of the lives
of the innocent unborn.
Change the hearts
of those who feel
they can't protect life
or those who don't see
the value in all life.
Help us build a community
that values life, liberty,
and the pursuit of happiness
for all.
Amen.

Take-Home

Make copies of today's closing prayer for the children to take home. Encourage them to lead their families in this prayer for the unborn, sick, and dying at least once this week.

C16: Caring for God's Community

Catechism: 1928–42

Objectives

- Begin to discover the foundations of the Church's teachings on social justice.
- List the seven themes of Catholic social teaching.
- Recognize how Christians stand up for the poor and vulnerable.

Leader Meditation

Luke 16:19–31

When have you felt like Lazarus and who cared for you? How can you respond to those like Lazarus in your world?

Leader Preparation

- Read the lesson, this lesson plan, the Scripture passage, and the *Catechism* sections.

Welcome

Greet the children as they arrive. Check for supplies and immediate needs. Solicit questions or comments about the previous session and/or share new information and findings. Begin promptly.

Opening Scripture

Luke 16:19–31

Light the candle and read aloud. Ask the children why they think the rich man might have ignored Lazarus and what he could have done for Lazarus when he was alive.

> The Church makes a moral judgment about economic and social matters, "when the fundamental rights of the person or the salvation of souls requires it."
>
> *CCC 2420*

Journey of Faith

Caring for God's Community

"I get that it's wrong if you're mean to people," said Tanya, "but how can you hurt or help people you've never even seen?"

"Jesus told a story about that," Mrs. Evans replied. "You can help everyone, even people you've never met, just by the way you live your life."

CCC 1928–42

Caring for God's Community

Discuss the reflection question as a group.

Responses will vary based on your group, but some possible responses include donating food or clothing even though you don't know the people who will benefit, regularly praying for all those in need, not being wasteful, treating everyone with kindness and respect, and so on.

Lazarus and the Rich Man

Ask the children to answer the reflection question with a partner or small group. Then ask each group to present their answer. Clarify any confusion or misunderstanding. Emphasize that this parable is meant to stress the importance of caring for everyone as our family in Christ. The rich man wasn't punished because God is vengeful and wanted him to suffer but because the rich man made choices, over and over again, to reject God and God's laws.

God Asks Us to Care

As you discuss the three ways the children can help care as God asks, try to offer concrete ways children can do these things in their community, through parish ministries, or at school. If the children are required to do community service before their confirmation, this is a great time to remind them or offer some suggestions of ways they can serve.

What do you think Mrs. Evans means?

Lazarus and the Rich Man

Once there was a rich man who wore expensive clothes and ate the best food every day. A beggar named Lazarus came to the rich man's house. Lazarus was so hungry he would have eaten the scraps from the rich man's table and been happy. But Lazarus' body was covered with sores, and he wasn't the kind of guest the rich man liked. So the rich man ignored him.

When Lazarus died, the angels took him to a place of honor next to Abraham in heaven. When the rich man died, he suffered terribly. When he saw Abraham and Lazarus, the rich man begged, "Have pity on me! Send Lazarus to give me just a drop of water! I'm burning up in this fire!"

Abraham answered, "Remember that while you lived, you had everything good and more than what you needed. Lazarus was sick, starving, and alone. You refused to help him. You ignored his pain. Now he is happy with God, and you are in pain."

Adapted from Luke 16:19–25

What can we learn from the story of Lazarus and the rich man?

God Asks Us to Care

The Church remembers that Jesus said, "The Lord has sent me to announce freedom for prisoners, to give sight to the blind, and to end everyone's suffering" (adapted from Luke 4:18).

Like Jesus, the Church cares when people are hungry, cold, or in pain. It cares when people are imprisoned or abused. When Church leaders hear about these injustices, they tell the world that these things are wrong and that it is up to us to stop them.

Jesus has a special love for the poor, needy, and suffering. Through his example and teachings, Jesus helps us understand why we have to care about the poor and suffering.

Here are three ways you can help:

1. Share what you have.

Like the five loaves and two fish discussed in Matthew 14:15–20, Mark 6:34–44, and Luke 9:12–17, God provides more than enough. It is up to us to pass on the extra and make sure people don't go without the things they need. We can share more than just our stuff, too. We can share what we know by telling others about God or teaching someone something we're really good at. We can share our joy by being nice to everyone.

SHARE

2. Help others all you can.

When Jesus washed his apostles' feet, he told them to do as he had done. His words and example tell us that our job as Christians is to serve others. He said, "Whoever wishes to be great among you shall be your servant; whoever wishes to be first among you shall be your slave" (Matthew 20:26–27). When we know someone is in need, Jesus wants us to help.

HELP

3. Stand up for what's right.

Whenever Jesus saw injustice, he stood firmly against it. At the Temple, he chased out the moneychangers who were getting rich by cheating people. He spoke against the teachers and leaders who were mixing up God's laws. He told people about their sins and helped them live more like him.

STAND UP FOR WHAT'S RIGHT

The pope and bishops have always spoken out against injustices. These are just some of the injustices we are asked to help make right.

The Economy

Everyone needs, and has the right to have, food, clothing, shelter, rest, medical care, education, and employment. The Church believes every country should make sure no person is denied these rights. Your parents or other adults might vote for laws that help people, and when you are old enough you can, too. But you can still do things now like sharing what you have or donating part of your allowance.

Family Life

The family is God's way of making sure that all children are loved and cared for. The Church believes that every country should support the family's right to grow and live in peace and safety and to pass on the faith and follow God.

Civil Rights

All people deserve to be treated equally. Laws should be written for the common good and enforced fairly. People should not be treated differently because of their appearance, age, gender, ability, or religion.

What are some things you can do to stand up for people who are in need or treated unfairly?

Civil Rights

Divide the children into pairs or small groups and ask them to answer the final reflection question together. Encourage them to come up with at least three different responses, one for each of the topics you discussed: the economy, family life, and civil rights.

When the children are finished, ask a spokesperson from each group to share responses with the class.

Share what you have. Does your parish hold clothing or canned-food drives year-round or during particular seasons? Is there an organization nearby that takes donations to help those in need? Does your parish have a day care or elementary school to which the children could donate gently used toys for younger children?

Help others all you can. Do the children have younger siblings they could help? Could they offer to take on additional chores when the rest of their family is extra-busy? Are there elderly members of the parish who could use help with yard work? Is there a retirement home accepting volunteers to make cards, perform holiday shows, or just spend time with residents? Can you put together cards and care packages for soldiers stationed away from home?

Stand up for what's right. Can the children find opportunities to avoid gossip? To stand up for a classmate being made fun of or bullied? Can they make choices to not engage in fights online or cyber-bullying? Does your parish offer a youth group for middle-school-age children or a prolife group for young persons?

Caring for God's Community

Final Activity

As you wrap up the lesson, give the children time to complete the final activity on their own. If you want to give the children more of a challenge, when they've finished matching the action to the way it helps, ask them to them write one or two sentences about why it fits into that category. Answers to the activity appear below.

How can we help?

Match the action to the way it helps people.

Your best friend really wants to get a part in the school play. You spend time helping him or her practice after school.

Your friends are talking about lying to their parents and sneaking into a movie and they want you to come. You decline.

You did a lot of extra chores this week so your dad gives you extra allowance! You want to spend it all, but instead you put some of it in the collection basket at church.

You know your mom is really busy, so you do dishes after dinner without being asked.

You overhear someone saying something mean and untrue about another person. You tell them that's wrong and they shouldn't spread rumors.

You notice a student in your class never has lunch to eat at lunchtime. You decide to pack a second sandwich to give to them at lunch.

Sharing what we have

Standing up for what's right

Helping others

In Short

- The foundations of Church teaching on social justice help all people.
- There are seven themes of Catholic social teaching.
- Christians stand up for the poor and vulnerable.

Journey of Faith for Children, Catechumenate, C16 (826344)
Imprimi Potest: Stephen T. Rehrauer, CSsR, Provincial, Denver Province, the Redemptorists.
Imprimatur: "In accordance with CIC 827, permission to publish has been granted on May 3, 2017, by Bishop Mark S. Rivituso, Vicar General, Archdiocese of St. Louis. Permission to publish is an indication that nothing contrary to Church teaching is contained in this work. It does not imply any endorsement of the opinions expressed in the publication, nor is any liability assumed by this permission."
Journey of Faith © 2000, 2017 Liguori Publications, Liguori, MO 63057. To order, visit Liguori.org or call 800-325-9521. Liguori Publications, a nonprofit corporation, is an apostolate of the Redemptorists. To learn more about the Redemptorists, visit Redemptorists.com. All rights reserved. No part of this publication may be reproduced, distributed, stored, transmitted, or posted in any form by any means without prior written permission.
Editors of the 2017 *Journey of Faith for Children:* Theresa Nienaber-Panuski and Pat Fosarelli, MD, DMin.
Design and production: Wendy Barnes, Lorena Mitre Jimenez, John Krus, and Bill Townsend. Illustration: Jeff Albrecht.
Unless noted, Scripture texts in this work are taken from the *New American Bible,* revised edition © 2000, 1991, 1986, 1970 Confraternity of Christian Doctrine, Washington, D.C., and are used by permission of the copyright owner. All Rights Reserved. No part of the *New American Bible* may be reproduced in any form without permission in writing from the copyright owner. Excerpts from the English translation of the *Catechism of the Catholic Church for the United States of America* © 1994 United States Catholic Conference, Inc.—*Libreria Editrice Vaticana;* English translation of the *Catechism of the Catholic Church: Modifications from the Editio Typica* © 1997 United States Catholic Conference, Inc.—*Libreria Editrice Vaticana.* Compliant with *The Roman Missal, Third Edition.*
Printed in the United States of America. 21 20 19 18 17 / 5 4 3 2 1. Third Edition.

Liguori PUBLICATIONS
A Redemptorist Ministry

Your best friend really wants to get a part in the school play. You spend time helping him or her practice after school.
Helping others.

Your friends are talking about lying to their parents and sneaking into a movie, and they want you to come. You say "no."
Standing up for what's right.

You did a lot of extra chores this week, so your dad gives you extra allowance! You want to spend it all, but instead, you put some of it in the collection basket at church.
Sharing what we have.

You know your mom is really busy, so you do the dishes after dinner without being asked.
Helping others.

You overhear people saying something mean and untrue about another person. You tell them that's wrong and they shouldn't spread rumors.
Standing up for what's right.

You notice a student in your class never has lunch to eat at lunchtime. You decide to pack a second sandwich to give to that child at lunch.
Sharing what we have.

Closing Prayer

Read Matthew 25:31–40, in which Jesus tells us that when we show care and concern for even the least of our brothers and sisters, we show love and concern for him. Ask for any special intentions after the reading and end by praying a Hail Mary together.

Take-Home

Sometimes it's easier to look away or not see the poor around us. For the next week, ask the children to really see the people around them by making eye contact and saying "hi" or by asking, "Do you need any help?" when they can.

Journey of Faith for Children
Catechumenate Glossary (alphabetical)

abortion: The intentional and deliberate destruction of a human fetus at any stage after conception. Abortion is an intrinsic evil both from the view of divine revelation and natural law ethics. The right to life is considered the most basic of all human rights, and the right to life of the unborn and innocent is inviolable.

absolve: In the sacrament of penance, this is the form, or words, spoken by the priest for the forgiveness of sins. Through the sign of absolution, God pardons the sinner who, in confession to the church's minister, has shared remorse for his or her sins and the desire to do better, which completes the sacrament of penance.

annulment: A pronouncement of the Church that a sacramental marriage never existed between two people.

anointed: During the sacrament of confirmation, the bishop will make a sign of the cross on the confirmand's head in holy oil as a physical sign that the Holy Spirit has come to dwell in the confirmand's heart.

anointing of the sick: A sacrament of healing that continues Jesus' healing ministry in the Church.

Book of the Elect: During the rite of election, those who desire to be Catholic write their names in this book to indicate their desire and to officially become a member of the elect (see **elect**).

candle (baptismal): Given to the newly baptized, this candle is lit from the paschal candle and symbolizes that Jesus is the light of the Church and the light for the newly baptized.

capital punishment: The decision of the state to put to death a person proven guilty of one or more serious crimes. The Church states that the death penalty should be carried out only in cases of absolute necessity, when it is impossible to protect society through any other means. As the organization of a penal system improves, cases where capital punishment is the only option become more rare, if not "practically nonexistent" (*Evangelium Vitae*, 56).

Church Fathers: Knowledgeable and faithful bishops and monks who helped early Christians understand their faith. Some of these early Church Fathers include Sts. Ignatius, Clement, Ambrose, Jerome, Basil, Gregory, and Augustine.

clergy: A term used to refer to men who have been ordained through the sacrament of holy orders.

commit: Promising to stick with something no matter what, or agreeing to see a task or obligation to completion.

confessional: The place in a church set aside for the celebration of the sacrament of penance. The penitent has the option of confessing to the priest face to face or anonymously behind a screen.

conscience: "Present at the heart of the person, enjoins him at the appropriate moment to do good and to avoid evil. It also judges particular choices, approving those that are good and denouncing those that are evil….It is a judgment of reason whereby the human person recognizes the moral quality of a concrete act that he is going to perform, is in the process of performing, or has already completed….It is by the judgment of his conscience that man perceives and recognizes the prescriptions of the divine law" (*CCC* 1777–78).

Constantine the Great: Ruler of the Roman Empire in the 300s, he was the first ruler to allow the legal practice of Christianity.

Constantinople: Now Istanbul, Turkey, Constantinople was once the center of the Eastern Orthodox Church.

Creed: A summary of the beliefs of any group, organization, or church. The Catholic Church has two creeds all members pray regularly: the Nicene Creed and the Apostles' Creed (see **Nicene Creed**).

curing: In the sacrament of anointing of the sick and in Jesus' ministry, this is the act of taking away a disease or physical disability.

Eastern Orthodox Church: A branch of the Church that separated in 1054 over disagreements about the role of the pope and teachings on the Holy Spirit.

elect: The name given to catechumens who have gone through the rite of election and who are preparing to celebrate baptism, confirmation, and the Eucharist at the next Easter Vigil.

Eucharist: This word means "thanksgiving." It is one of the sacraments of the Church and is the source and summit of all Christian worship and life. The sacrament of the Eucharist was instituted by Jesus at the Last Supper and is celebrated by the Church today as a representation of Jesus' sacrifice on the cross for our sins. During the Eucharist, the offering of bread and wine becomes the precious Body and Blood of Christ.

euthanasia: "An action or an omission which of itself and by intention causes death, in order that all suffering may in this way be eliminated" (Declaration on Euthanasia). This act is considered morally wrong in all cases, even when the patient may request it, as it is a crime against life and the dignity of the human person. Euthanasia should not be confused with the refusal of extraordinary means of care, which a patient may refuse in conscience. For a more precise differentiation between these two, see *Evangelium Vitae*.

healing: In the sacrament of anointing of the sick and in Jesus' healing ministry, this is the act of strengthening the recipient's soul and giving the person the courage to face and be at peace with the trials ahead, whether that is continued illness, a cure, or death.

holy oil: Used during anointing of the sick as a physical symbol preparing the sick person for the Holy Spirit.

holy orders: A sacrament where men pledge their lives to God through service of God's Church.

laying on of hands: A sign that the Holy Spirit has been invited to live in us. It is used as a symbol during the sacrament of confirmation.

Martin Luther: A former Catholic monk and priest who, in the 1500s, saw mistakes being made in the Church. He wanted to work with the Church to correct these mistakes, but he eventually left the Church and became the founder of Lutheran Church.

missionaries: People who go out to spread the good news of Jesus' death and resurrection, and of his presence in the Church to those who would not otherwise hear it. Traditionally missionaries traveled to foreign countries, but anyone who actively evangelizes the good news of Jesus and his Church can be considered a missionary. In fact, the Church's very nature is missionary.

neophyte: In the context of the RCIA, one who has been "newly planted" in the faith through the sacrament of baptism; a newly baptized Catholic Christian.

Nicene Creed: The creed most often used during Sunday Mass (see **Creed**).

oil of chrism: Used during the sacraments of baptism, confirmation, and during the ordination of a priest or bishop.

ordained: When priestly authority is passed down, through the laying on of hands, from one generation to the next. Ordination takes place during the sacrament of holy orders, which has three forms: the diaconate (deacons), priesthood (priests), and the episcopate (bishops).

penance: Given before the prayer of absolution during the sacrament of penance and reconciliation, this is an act through which the penitent shows remorse for his or her sins and attempts to right any wrongs they've committed and mend any damage to their relationships with others and God.

Pentecost: A liturgical solemnity celebrated fifty days after Easter to commemorate the descent of the Holy Spirit on the apostles and the baptism of an estimated 3,000 new Christians (Acts 2:1–41). It recognizes and celebrates the missionary nature of the Church through the Holy Spirit.

permanent deacon: A married or unmarried man who is ordained a deacon and remains a deacon permanently. To become a permanent deacon a man must be (1) qualified, unmarried, and twenty-five years of age or older or (2) qualified, married, and age thirty-five or older with the consent of his wife. Once ordained a permanent deacon, a man cannot marry (if unmarried) or remarry (if married).

persecute: Under the rule of the Roman Empire, this meant early Christians were arrested, hurt, or killed because of their religious beliefs.

plagues: In Exodus, these were the ten plights God sent to Egypt before the Pharaoh agreed to free the Israelites from slavery. The ten plagues were: water turned to blood, frogs, biting insects, wild animals, diseased livestock, boils, a storm of hail and fire, locusts, three days of darkness, and the death of all firstborn males.

poverty: A state where someone does not have access to or the ability to buy items necessary for their basic needs, like food, clean water, or shelter.

prejudiced: A preconceived notion of someone or some group of people that is commonly based on stereotypes rather than actual experience.

Protestant: A name given to those churches that were created during the schism from the Catholic Church because these groups were protesting what was going on in the Church at the time.

religious orders: Groups of men and women who live together and focus on a specific spirituality or way of serving God. Some religious orders today are the Jesuits, Franciscans, Redemptorists, and Dominicans. They teach in schools, help in hospitals, preach to people, and live lives of prayer.

rite of acceptance: The rite through which an inquirer becomes a catechumen. During this rite, the inquirer states his or her intention to become a baptized member of the Catholic Church amidst the parish community. The community then affirms the inquirer's desire, and the inquirer officially becomes a catechumen.

---

rite of election: A candidate or catechumen is accepted to receive the sacraments of initiation or their decision to choose the Catholic Church is accepted.

rite of initiation: Held during the Easter Vigil Mass, this is the rite where the sacraments of initiation are received and candidates and catechumens become neophytes in the Church (see **sacraments of initiation** and **neophyte**).

rite of welcoming: Those inquirers who have been previously baptized, but who have not received any other sacraments, become candidates in the RCIA process through this rite.

Roman Empire: The ruling government during the time of the early Church. The Roman Empire was pagan and felt the early Church was threatening its power, so it would persecute members of the early Church.

sacrament: A sign and instrument by which the Holy Spirit spreads the grace of Christ throughout the Church, his body. The Church celebrates seven sacraments: baptism, penance and reconciliation, the Eucharist, confirmation, holy orders, marriage, and anointing of the sick.

sacraments of initiation: The sacraments received to become a full member of the Catholic Church: baptism, confirmation, and the Eucharist.

sacrament of matrimony: The sacrament where a man and woman, groom and bride, are joined together so closely they become one, accepting the blessing and responsibility of raising new life in the Church.

schism: A split or division. When referencing Church history, this refers to the split from the original, unified Church into a number of denominations.

scrutinies: Three additional rites during the third, fourth, and fifth Sundays of Lent for the unbaptized elect. The purpose of these scrutinies is to examine one's life and to reflect on personal sin through the light of God's mercy and grace.

sponsor: It is the sponsor's role to offer support and encouragement during the RCIA process and then to present the candidate when it is time for him or her to receive the sacraments. The requirements for a sponsor are the same as for a godparent.

substance: In a spiritual context, substance describes what God is, a being whose essence requires that it exist in itself rather than a being that exists in or because of another.

Ten Commandments: God's laws given by God to Moses on Mount Sinai and interpreted by Jesus Christ.

transitional deacon: A man who receives the order of deacon as he advances to the priesthood.

Vatican II: A meeting of Catholic bishops, laypeople, and leaders from other Christian communities called in 1959 by Pope John XXIII. Among many matters, this meeting focused on the importance of laypeople in the Church, the importance of studying the Bible, working peacefully with other religions to promote social justice, and celebrating the Mass in the language of the people.

vows: During the sacrament of matrimony, these are the promises the bride and groom make to each other before God and their witnesses.

water: Used during the sacrament of baptism, this is a sign that all our sins are washed away in Christ and we become reborn in the Church.

wedding rings: A physical symbol used in the sacrament of matrimony to symbolize the couple's everlasting bond.

Western (Latin) Church: The modern-day Catholic Church, the center of which is in Vatican City in Rome, Italy.

white garment: The newly baptized are clothed in this to symbolize they have become a new person, wrapped in Jesus Christ.